JESUS AND
THE GOSPEL TRADITION

SPCK Large Paperbacks

JESUS AND
THE GOSPEL TRADITION

C. K. BARRETT

LONDON
S · P · C · K

First published in 1967
First paperback edition 1975
Third impression 1977
SPCK
Holy Trinity Church
Marylebone Road
London NW1 4DU

Printed in Great Britain by
Hollen Street Press Limited
Slough, Berkshire

2198/12

ISBN 0 281 02821 4

Contents

Acknowledgements

Thanks are due to the following for permission to quote from copyright sources:

Walter de Gruyter & Co.: *On the Trial of Jesus*, by P. Winter.

Nicholson & Watson Ltd and Charles Scribner's Sons: *Jesus and the Word*, by Rudolf Bultmann.

Preface

This book contains the Shaffer Lectures, which I delivered at Yale University Divinity School in April 1965. Much of the material was subsequently used, in July 1966, in lectures in the Faculty of Theology at Hamburg University.

A lecturer on the Shaffer foundation must deal with some aspect of the life and work of Jesus. This is a stiff, indeed an impossible, assignment; yet, however my predecessors in the lectureship may have reacted to the task that was laid upon them, I welcomed it, not because I felt competent to discharge it, but because I knew it would make me face questions from which for years I had been running away. When a critical student of the New Testament says the word "Jesus" he raises at least two questions: a historical question, and a theological question. First, what do we really know, as historians, about Jesus? Did he really say this? Did he really do that? And secondly, if our historical knowledge of Jesus is in any way limited or uncertain, how is our theological estimate of him affected? How far is our present relationship with the exalted Lord Jesus conditioned by or dependent upon historical research into the records of the earthly life of Jesus of Nazareth? It is possible, in the course of routine teaching, to sidestep these questions; where the first is concerned, to list the answers of a dozen authorities, and play them off against one another, and then to treat the second in a dependent conditional pronouncement—if so-and-so, then this und that. This sort of procedure may, perhaps, be useful to one's hearers in day-to-day lecturing, but it is not good enough as a response to an undeserved but flattering invitation to cross the Atlantic and declare one's views on a great subject.

This small book represents, then, in the first instance, an attempt to clear my own mind on a number of issues in regard to which I have for a long time held my judgement in suspense. The process of clarification has, I hope, been kept in the background; I have tried to present only trains of thought that I could bring to something like a conclusion, and I have found, as one often does, that one conclusion, drawn with reasonable confidence, leads to the solution of other problems which at first seemed less tractable. It has of course been impossible to go into detail, but, after some hesitation, I have decided that the right course is to publish the lectures more or less as they were given (though, both at New Haven and at Hamburg, I had to omit much that I had written), rather than to inflate them by discussing every point in full, and multiplying references to those to whom I am indebted—whether in agreement or dis-agreement.

It will not, I think, be disputed that the questions I have asked are important, or that they arise out of the New Testament itself—this is the real point of pp. 1f. The adequacy of the answers is another matter, and I should like here not only to acknowledge the many inadequacies that are due simply to my own incompetence, but also to draw attention to the Postscript (pp. 103–8), which recognizes, even if it fails to remove, a serious deficiency which is inherent in the plan of the under-taking itself.

It remains only to express the warmest possible thanks to the Shaffer Trustees who invited me to be their lecturer; to the Dean of Yale Divinity School and his colleagues, whose gene-rous hospitality and friendship made my short stay with them a pleasurable memory; also to Professor Goppelt, and his col-leagues, who invited me to Hamburg and welcomed me there. A debt to German New Testament scholarship accumulated over thirty years is not to be discharged in the compass of a week, but it is good to have had the opportunity of acknowledging it.

I must thank also those who have contributed to the substance of the lectures. During the last few years I have discussed the "Son of man" sayings in the gospels with Dr M. D. Hooker and Dr M. E. Glasswell so often that I sometimes find it difficult to know which ideas were originally mine, and which theirs. The reader will be safe in concluding that the brightest ideas were theirs, but he must not, without further evidence, saddle them with responsibility for any views I have expressed.

I am also grateful to Miss C. E. Adams, who, by reducing to typescript the longhand manuscript from which I lectured at Yale, made it easier for me to make a German version for Hamburg, and to revise the text for publication.

Durham,   C. K. BARRETT
July 1966.

1

The Tradition

In the opening paragraph of 1 Corinthians 15 Paul is concerned to establish that, at least in the central proposition that Jesus of Nazareth, once crucified, had now been raised from the dead, there was no difference between himself and other bearers of the apostolic Gospel. "Whether then it was I or they, so we preach, and so you believed" (1 Cor. 15.11). In establishing this point he draws attention to the existence of a Christian tradition, and also states its two essential components.

The idea of tradition cannot be expressed more clearly than it is in the words, "I delivered to you that which also I received" (1 Cor. 15.3). The words are drawn from the technical language of tradition, for behind *delivered* and *received* stand the Greek παρέδωκα and παρέλαβον, and behind these in turn the rabbinic words מסר and קבל. The truth transmitted was the foundation of faith. Paul had not evolved a religion out of his own consciousness, nor was he content (though doubtless many of his correspondents would have been) that Corinthian Christianity should consist simply in the effervescence of spiritual excitement. Objective and (in some sense)[1] verifiable historical truths

---

[1] The point of Paul's list of witnesses in 1 Cor. 15.5–8 is disputed. See R. Bultmann, *Glauben und Verstehen* I, 1933, 54f. But the list would be meaningless if Paul were not thinking of genuine experiences concerning which those who received them might be interrogated. "There can be

had, first in him and then in them, evoked response. Beneath the various expressions of Christian faith was a factual basis, which one generation could repeat to another.

This basis consisted of two primary facts: first, that Christ had died (1 Cor. 15.3), and, second, that he had been raised from the dead (1 Cor. 15.4). The tradition Paul quotes not only stated these as historical facts, but also provided them with a rudimentary theological interpretation, adding to the bare statement that Christ died the qualifications that he died "for our sins" and "according to the Scriptures", providing the assertion of the resurrection with the same scriptural context, and significantly putting the verb in the passive—for "he has been raised" implies an active verb of which the subject is God: "God raised him from the dead" (cf. Rom. 10.9).

We are not about to study 1 Corinthians for its own sake. The point is this. When Paul (innocently enough) wrote out the first paragraph of 1 Corinthians 15, with its reference to the primitive tradition and its two poles, crucifixion and resurrection, he stated in advance three themes which between them go far towards crystallizing the study of Jesus as this proceeds in the latter half of the twentieth century. These three themes will provide the subjects of our lectures:

1. The Tradition
2. Christ Crucified
3. Christ to Come

These may be expanded as follows. (1) What were the contents, and what were the purpose and the method, of the primitive tradition about Jesus? In particular, how is the ostensible history contained in the tradition related to the avowed theological interests of the early Church? (2) How is the preached, theological interpretation of Jesus' death related to the

---

no demonstration of the event [the resurrection] which has apologetic value, and no such demonstration is attempted in 1 Cor. 15. All the same, 1 Cor. 15 shows that within the circle of disciples there was a firm tradition in respect of this witness" (K. Barth, *Church Dogmatics* IV, 2, 1958, p. 143).

historical event and to Jesus' own understanding of it? (3) Granted that, after Jesus' death on a Friday, his disciples on the following Sunday became convinced that he himself was alive and in communication with them, and that they were living in a new period of world history: granted all this, how did this Easter faith square with Jesus' own teaching about the future, and how did it give rise to the Church's life and message?

The three themes interlock, but they are separable, and we shall proceed at once with the first. In one of the greatest courses of lectures ever given in America by a British scholar, Gilbert Murray spoke of Homer's *Iliad* as follows:

> If you take up the *Iliad* as a record of history, you will soon put it down as so much mere poetry. But if you read it as fiction you will at every page be pulled up by the feeling that it is not free fiction. The poet does not invent whatever he likes. He believes himself to be dealing with real events and real people, to be recording and explaining things that have value, primarily, because they are supposed to be true.[2]

This double aspect of the Greek Epic, as Murray made unforgettably clear, is due not to the irresponsible injection of poetic fancy into historical tradition, nor to the indiscriminate scattering of a few historical plums into the poetical pudding, but to the crossing of two genuine historical contexts, the mingling of past and present in the hands of men who were not provided with the discriminatory tools of historical scholarship, and would probably in any case have preferred a poetic synthesis to a scientific dissection of diverse historical materials. It is not necessary to believe the whole of the traditional story about Helen (who appears in fact to have been a marriage-*kore* in Sparta)[3] in order to see in the *Iliad* some kind of record of tribal customs and migrations, and even of tribal leaders; but these prehistoric events and ways are seen refracted through the circumstances of a different period, in which new political institutions, military methods, social habits, and economic

---

[2] G. Murray, *The Rise of the Greek Epic*, 4th edn., 1934, p. 173.
[3] Murray, op. cit., p. 205.

structures prevailed. In addition, the poets view the past with genuine poetic emotion, and with pious and patriotic sentiments.

These observations may lead us to the gospels, encouraged by the sense that the problems we encounter there are not wholly new. Though in matters of detail opinions would differ widely, most would, I think, agree that Murray's comment on the *Iliad* could be applied to the gospels. Thus, if you begin by reading the gospels as history you are soon impressed by their unhistorical character. I do not propose to illustrate at length a conclusion that is sufficiently familiar.

There is, for example, little need to speak of the supernatural and mythical element in the gospels. This in itself means little more than that the gospels were written in the ancient rather than the modern world; though it is reasonable to add that they lack the healthy rational scepticism of ancient writers such as Thucydides, Tacitus, or Lucian. No modern reader, however conservative, can honestly profess to feel at home in a world where heavenly doves descend and supernatural voices speak, a world of transfigurations and nature miracles, of angels and demons. It would be bad historical method to rule out *a priori* the possible historicity of all such events, but no one who takes up a gospel looking for what he understands as history can be reassured by the frequency with which the supernatural appears. It does not so appear in his own experience.

We come nearer to the point with the observation that, if the gospels are historical at all, they convey only episodic history. Their connectedness lies simply in the centrality of one person, Jesus, and it is not possible to trace lines of psychological or other development even in him. No attempt is made to suggest any progression in his thought and teaching; what he says at the beginning he says also at the end. Corresponding to this is the fact that the opposition of the Jews is represented as having reached an extreme stage as early as Mark 3.6,[4] while Jesus himself continues to act as a devout Jew as late as Mark 11.16,

---

[4] And cf. 2.7 with 14.64; the final charge of blasphemy is stated at the beginning of the gospel.

where he refuses to permit the use of the Temple as a thorough-fare.[5]

Within the episodes formidable historical difficulties arise; these will be sufficiently illustrated as we proceed, and I need not linger over examples now. The difficulties become more acute still when we compare the gospel narratives. We cannot, for example, believe both that James and John asked Jesus to grant them the first places in his glory (Mark 10.35ff.), and that their mother made the request for them (Matt. 20.20f.).

Thus a critical reader, approaching the gospels as historical documents, will find the most favourable verdict he can pass to be that, if they are history at all, they are certainly not history as he would have written it. They leave his questions un-answered, are often inconsistent with one another and with the historical background presupposed by their story, and they manifest a naive credulity that evokes anything but confidence.

If, however, the reader approaches the gospels with the assumption that they are fictitious he is equally likely to find himself contradicted. At the threshold of Mark he finds an account of the baptism of Jesus by John. This story was found so difficult and scandalous by the early Church that Luke[6] passes it by in a participial clause, Matthew[7] adds a short ex-planatory conversation between Jesus and the Baptist, John omits the incident altogether, and the Gospel according to the Hebrews[8] grasps the nettle by putting on the lips of Jesus the direct challenge, *Quid peccavi?* No one invented this story. The reader may perhaps conclude that certain features such as the dove, the voice from heaven, and the adoption formula, "Thou art my son", are all so much jam for the pill, designed to make it possible for Christians to stomach the unpalatable; but he will find it hard to shake the narrative framework. This is history as it happened.

[5] There is a similar prohibition in Berakoth 9.5.
[6] 3.21, βαπτισθέντος (having been baptized).
[7] 3.14f.
[8] Jerome, *Contra Pelagianos* III.2: "What sin have I committed, that I should go and be baptized by him? Unless indeed this very thing that I have said is [a sin of] ignorance."

2

Again, the reader will observe that though the early Church thought of Jesus as Messiah, Son of God, Wisdom, and Word, these titles, so far as they appear at all, are by no means prominent in the teaching of Jesus as the gospels record it. Instead, Jesus frequently speaks of a figure whom he calls the Son of man, a title that (with the exception of Acts 7.56) the early Church scarcely used until it had forgotten its meaning.[9] The question whether Jesus used the title, and whether, if he did, he used it of himself, is one we ought to be careful not to prejudge; but it is fair to say that there is a *prima facie* case for the view that when we meet it in the gospels we encounter fact rather than fiction.

This observation will lead us further. "The Son of man" is a very odd English phrase; and ὁ υἱὸς τοῦ ἀνθρώπου is very odd Greek. But בר נשא is good Aramaic, and the fact may remind the reader that there is not a little of the language of the gospels that can be put back into Semitic word or sentence structure. This observation can never prove that the words in question were spoken by Jesus—he was only one among many who spoke Aramaic; but at least it suggests that the evangelists, who wrote in Greek, were not freely inventing. The same may be said of details of Palestinian life which are reflected, some in the parables, others in the stories about Jesus. The gospels as they stand are not essentially Jewish works, for their literary environment and background are Hellenistic.[10] Yet they are not the free composition of Hellenistic writers, but are based upon material some of which is Semitic and Palestinian in origin.

The conclusion we have reached, that the gospels are neither pure history nor pure fiction, is sufficiently evident. It has long

---

[9] Later evangelists occasionally introduce the title into contexts that did not originally contain it, but this is no more than editorial extension of earlier usage. The use of "Son of man" constitutes one of the most difficult of New Testament problems, and has recently been discussed in several excellent monographs and articles, which have, however, by no means achieved unanimity. It will arise several times in this book.

[10] Biography and romance are Hellenistic rather than Jewish literary forms, though there are examples of both in the Old Testament.

been recognized. But it gives rise to problems that have not yet been solved. What was the role of historical tradition in primitive Christianity? We have no ground for thinking that the early Church was interested in biography for its own sake; we have every reason to think that its faith and its theology were focused upon Jesus as the Lord in heaven. Why then was historical tradition about the earthly life of Jesus of Nazareth preserved, and how did it come to be preserved in the form in which we have it?[11]

The old answer to these questions was that natural, untheological events were impregnated with, and obscured by, a stream of theology that was essentially foreign to them. Jesus was a man who had taught his fellows to live as brothers under the rule of their heavenly Father, but Paul, and others, had thrust him into the categories of rabbinic and hellenistic speculation, introducing into the gospels mythological ideas of incarnation and of atonement through the shedding of blood, and aetiological legends justifying their own cult practices. This answer has the attractiveness of its simplicity, but it has long been known that it does not meet the facts.[12] Such a process of theologizing, if it occurred at all, must have been unbelievably thorough, pervasive, and early, for however the gospel material is analysed, whether by source criticism into such units as Mk, Q, M, and L, or by form criticism into aphorisms, parables, tales, paradigms, and so forth, no analytical unit can be found which is not essentially theological in character. The fact that the theologies of the various units differ among themselves only makes crude theologizing more improbable. Further, the process by which an undogmatic Jesus was recovered from the

---

[11] In an earlier generation Scott Holland (and few others) perceived the enigma of the synoptic gospels. "They give no account of themselves. They raise problems for which they offer no solution. They provoke questions which they never attempt to answer. They leave off at a point where it is impossible to stop" (*The Fourth Gospel*, 1923, p. 2). It is true, however, that the problems do not look quite the same to-day.

[12] See especially E. C. Hoskyns, "The Christ of the Synoptic Gospels" in *Essays Catholic and Critical*, ed. E. G. Selwyn, 1926, pp. 151–78; E. Hoskyns and N. Davey, *The Riddle of the New Testament*, 1931, especially pp. 111–207.

sources has been shown to be historically unsound. Not only are the sources themselves theologically motivated, the story they tell is also theologically motivated. For example, Albert Schweitzer[13] demonstrated the significance of eschatology as a motive in the story of Jesus. It is doubtful whether any one to-day would accept all Schweitzer's conclusions, but the main point stands; the story as a whole is controlled by eschatology, and eschatology is theology. It is not the only theological theme in the gospels, and its centrality has been challenged.[14] The position is a complicated one. But precisely this is the point. It is impossible to separate out of the gospels a simple, uncomplicated, historical tale, free of theological interest.

All this has long been recognized. The conclusion was greeted with relief by theologians and churchmen, who were perhaps a little premature in celebrating the overthrow of a purely humanist interpretation[15] of Jesus; but it raises a problem for the historian. If we could think of a theological tradition about Jesus (attested mainly by Paul, who shows practically no interest in the history of Jesus), and a historical tradition about Jesus, then, even if we had to think of the contamination of the latter by the former, the position would be relatively simple. It seems, however, that we have to think of two theological traditions, or at least of a theological tradition, and of a tradition both historical and theological. How could such traditions be related to each other?

A recent development in gospel study virtually identifies them. I refer to the view of New Testament tradition adumbrated first by Harald Riesenfeld,[16] and worked out in detail (though not yet over the whole field) by Birger Gerhardsson.[17]

---

[13] See especially *The Mystery of the Kingdom of God*, 1925.

[14] See E. Bammel, "Erwägungen zur Eschatologie Jesu" in *Studia Evangelica III*, 1964, *Texte und Untersuchungen* 88, pp. 3–32.

[15] The problem of "the historical Jesus" has became not less but more acute. See pp. 87f.

[16] *The Gospel Tradition and its Beginnings*, 1957.

[17] *Memory and Manuscript*, 1961; *Tradition and Transmission in Early Christianity*, 1964. I may refer to my reviews in *Journal of Theological Studies*, new series xiv, 1963, pp. 445–9; xvi, 1965, pp. 488f.

This view, though its authors do not allow the fact, is essentially
a distinctive variation of the form-critical approach familiar
since the 1920's, but instead of finding the natural setting for
the gospel material within the preaching of the early Church,
and in its controversial, ethical, and liturgical activities, they
place it within a traditionary process comparable with that
which can be traced (and has been traced by Dr Gerhardsson
with great care and accuracy) within contemporary Judaism.
This process originated with Jesus himself, who taught his
disciples and made them learn his message, together with his
interpretation of some of the events that befell him, by heart.
After Jesus' death and resurrection this message was remembered as a ἱερὸς λόγος, a sacred word that constituted both the
preaching and the organized and disciplined life of the Christian
community. Its approved guardians and expositors were the
apostles, who thus exercised, and were recognized as exer-
cising, great authority over the life and thought of the Church.
When, in Acts 6.4, they are described as devoting themselves
to the "ministry of the word", this refers not, as has generally
been supposed, to preaching, but to the transmission and development of the holy tradition.

This theory makes it possible to conceive the unity of the
New Testament in a way that has seemed excluded since the
rise of critical scholarship. All springs from the teaching of
Jesus, and developments of that teaching were carefully super-
vised by those whom he had himself appointed for the purpose,
men whose authority was recognized (for example) by Paul, so
that Paul's own theological teaching may be understood as
legitimately continuous with that of Jesus. Unfortunately, the
picture presented to us corresponds neither to what we know
of the early Church, nor to what we may deduce from the
gospels themselves about Jesus. It is true that, in the gospels,
Jesus is not infrequently addressed as rabbi, and his activities
no doubt bore some resemblance to those of regular Jewish
teachers. There is, however, no indication that he conducted
his ministry on the lines of instruction practised in a rabbinic
school; rather the contrary. He does not praise his disciples

(when he is able to praise them at all) as being like "plastered cisterns, losing not a drop" (cf. Aboth 2.8). In a neglected note in *The Teaching of Jesus*, T. W. Manson argued, not conclusively but with a good deal of force, that the word used by Jesus to describe his disciples was not תלמידא (*talmida*) but שוליא (*sh'wilya*); that is, they were not so much students as apprentices.

> It is tempting to see in the choice of the word a definite opposition to the whole scribal system. . . . The life of a *talmid* as *talmid* was made up of study of the sacred writings, attendance on lectures, and discussion of difficult passages or cases. Discipleship as Jesus conceived it was not a theoretical discipline of this sort, but a practical task to which men were called to give themselves and all their energies. Their work was not study but practice . . . .[18]

It would be wrong to press this point too far; but, though Dr Gerhardsson would not have us build on Mark 1.22,27 (which contrast the authority of Jesus with that of the scribes), these passages are symptomatic of the belief of the evangelists, and, we may say, of earlier bearers of the tradition also, that the tradition originated rather in the impression made by a charismatic person[19] than in sayings learnt by rote. Especially when the different forms in which sayings occur in the various gospel sources are borne in mind it is difficult to accept the notion of a fixed and authoritative sacred word. There was no degree of fixation sufficient to interfere with the editorial activity of the evangelists and their predecessors, and this activity was not confined to the exposition and application of given material.

When we turn to the rest of the New Testament we find little evidence for the kind of apostolic activity Dr Gerhardsson describes. He paints for us a picture of an apostolic college situated in Jerusalem, studying the sacred tradition, and issuing on the basis of it authorized interpretations, exegesis of Old

[18] T. W. Manson, *The Teaching of Jesus*, 1935, p. 239.
[19] Cf. R. Otto, *The Kingdom of God and the Son of Man*, 1938, especially pp. 351, 379. To put the matter in this way, however, runs the risk of simply transferring Jesus from the category of the rabbis to that of the prophets, whereas, according to the evangelists, he belongs properly to neither.

Testament scripture, and rules for the government of church life. Acts 15, for example, is said to show us a picture of the college at work, issuing its decree. The formulation of such a decree is an example of the "ministry of the word" (Acts 6.4). But this is not a convincing account of the facts. We have no precise knowledge of what the apostles did in Jerusalem. Luke, writing towards the end of the first century, and evidently on the basis of very scanty knowledge, does his best to represent the Twelve as an impressive central body, but he tells us nothing of what they did, can only associate them with a few incidents he is able to report concerning Peter and John, and even so soon loses interest in them. For a variety of reasons, which cannot be given in detail here,[20] it is impossible to accept as it stands the account of the Council in Acts 15, though there may be some historical material behind it. At least, the "Decree" seems to have had no validity in Galatia and Achaea. On the contrary, Paul energetically discounted the authority of the Jerusalem apostles; he had nothing to learn from the "Pillars", and when emissaries from James scared Peter off the right path, Paul had no hesitation in telling the great guarantor of the sacred tradition exactly what he thought of him (Gal. 2.6f.,11).

It is true, and important, that Paul's attitude to Jerusalem, and the Jerusalem apostles, was complex. Difficult though the situation was (and how difficult can be shown only by a detailed examination of 2 Corinthians 10—13),[21] he did his best to avoid an open and complete break with the Judean Church, and this may have been in part because he felt the need of the historical tradition of which that Church was the repository. But this is not likely.[22] Concerned as Paul was with the historical fact of Jesus, he shows scant concern with the historical tradition about him, quoting (in addition to the Last Supper material) one saying about divorce, one about the payment of

[20] See E. Haenchen, *Die Apostelgeschichte*, 1965, pp. 396–414.
[21] See, e.g., E. Käsemann, "Die Legitimität des Apostels", in *Zeitschrift für die neutestamentliche Wissenschaft* 41, 1942, pp. 33–71.
[22] He valued them as witnesses to the resurrection: 1 Cor. 15.5–8.

ministers, and one about the *parousia*.[23] It is a very important datum of our problem that Paul did not go out of his way to use the historical material that Jerusalem could (perhaps) supply. Though he could speak of the "law of Christ" (Gal. 6.2; cf. 1 Cor. 9.21) he had no intention of permitting this requirement of love to become, through the multiplication of new *halakoth*, a new legalism. His anxiety not to break off relations with the mother Church turned, very probably, upon his concern for the conversion of Israel.

Dr Riesenfeld and Dr Gerhardsson have rightly emphasized the fact, too much neglected, that, especially among Jews, tradition was a technical process whose methods were well understood and carefully practised. We need not doubt that when Jewish Christians thought fit to memorize and transmit material word for word they would be able to do so with a considerable measure of accuracy. But it remains to be proved that the early Church as a whole wished to do this, and that Jesus intended it. Historical tradition was handed down (a fact for which the Pauline epistles do not prepare us), but it was handed down (as comparative study of the gospels shows) in the context of free interpretation, and not with a concern for verbal accuracy. It is still true that we are confronted, in primitive Christianity, with two traditions, one the almost purely theological tradition that we meet in Paul, the other the curious mingling of historical recollection and theological conviction that we encounter in the gospels; and we have so far been able neither to identify them, nor to explain the relation between them.

There is more help for us in the process now commonly referred to as *Redaktionsgeschichte*[24] (redaction criticism), which has rightly exalted the evangelists from the position into which form criticism had tended to depress them. They are not to be thought of as mere collectors of material. They wrote (not,

---

[23] 1 Cor. 7.10; 9.14; 1 Thess. 4.15. In other passages (e.g. Rom. 13.9) Paul may echo words of Jesus, but does not indicate that he is doing so.

[24] See W. Marxsen, *Der Evangelist Markus*, 1956; also H. Conzelmann, *The Theology of St Luke*, 1960, and G. Bornkamm, G. Barth, and H. J. Held, *Tradition and Interpretation in Matthew*, 1963.

perhaps, as individuals, but as representatives of a wider group) with their own theological and practical interests which the traditional material was compelled to serve, partly by direct modification, partly by the way in which it was arranged and different pieces combined with one another. Here we may see a further point at which theological interpretation affected the historical tradition. As Willi Marxsen says,[25] "If J. Jeremias distinguishes the 'first *Sitz im Leben*', which is to be found in the unique situation of the activity of Jesus, from the 'second *Sitz im Leben*', which is provided by the situation of the primitive Church and which form criticism seeks to make known, then what we are now concerned with is the 'third *Sitz im Leben*'"— that is, the setting which provides the explanatory context for the evangelist's own work. Dr Marxsen points out, rightly, that at this point form criticism and redaction criticism stand very close together; in fact it is questionable whether we ought to speak of a "third *Sitz im Leben*". Naturally, there were in fact very many different settings; that in which a saying (whether authentic or not) was used in Palestine in the 30's was very different from that in which, for example, Luke wrote. But if we are to count settings in this way, we shall reach, not three, but an infinite number, most of which we shall be unable to describe accurately or differentiate usefully. It is perhaps better to recognize in the study of tradition, which we call *Formgeschichte*, and in the study of the construction of the gospels, which we call *Redaktionsgeschichte*, two different ways of taking into account the "second *Sitz im Leben*", of which there is only one significant definition: the time after the death and resurrection of Jesus.[26]

---

[25] Op. cit., p. 12.
[26] There is an important distinction to make here, but it is not tied to the distinction between oral tradition and written redaction. The historical tradition about Jesus was subjected to two great disturbances, which gave rise to two distinguishable settings subsequent to the first (that in the ministry of Jesus). The first occurred when the ministry of Jesus issued in his death and resurrection, and (unexpectedly) the continuing life of disciples in this age, the second when the consummation failed to take place within the first generation of Christians.

It is at this point that we return to the observations of Gilbert Murray. Greek epic gives the appearance either of history with a strong imaginative element, or of fiction with a deep strain of history in it, because it arises from the interaction of two (or more) historical periods, under the catalytic effect of the poetic fancy and patriotic sentiment. We may begin with a similar observation about the gospels, which contain very little that is not historical in some sense. Material that does not reflect the ministry of Jesus reflects the life of the primitive Church; some material reflects both. Our difficulty arises from the fact that though these two historical contexts sometimes lie side by side, like two threads, which patience and care can disentangle and separate from each other, at other times they mingle like two streams that have flowed into each other to make one river.

A good example of the way in which two historical contexts can be laid bare and distinguished from each other is provided by Joachim Jeremias's analysis of the parable of the Sower and its interpretation (Mark 4.3–8, 13–20).[27] The parable itself is only intelligible on the basis of the Palestinian custom of sowing before ploughing; apart from this the sower's action is bound to appear foolish. Why should he waste good seed on the field path, the patch of thorns, the stony stretch of soil? But not only is the detail of the parable authentically Palestinian, and derived in all probability from Jesus' own observation, the thought of the parable fits into the context of Jesus' eschatological message as this can be reconstructed from other sources. This parable belongs (if we may say this of any piece of gospel material) to the teaching of Jesus. With the interpretation, however, it is otherwise. The language itself, and the circumstances of persecution, and worldly cares which threaten the success of the preaching of the word, point to the history of the Church. Here we may claim that the two strands lie side by side, and

[27] J. Jeremias, *The Parables of Jesus*, 1963, pp. 13f., 77ff., 149ff. Interesting criticisms have been made by K. D. White (*Journal of Theological Studies*, new series xv, pp. 300–7), but he too concludes, "The Sower is represented as behaving in the way in which any competent Mediterranean farmer of the period would normally behave" (p. 307).

bear witness respectively to the story of Jesus and the story of his followers in the time after his death and resurrection.

It is different when we turn to the notoriously obscure verses that intervene between the parable and its interpretation (Mark 4.10ff.). Time would scarcely permit me even to list the interpretations and critical evaluations of these verses that have been offered within the present generation of New Testament scholarship. I will illustrate my point with a few observations that fall in pairs. (1) As T. W. Manson observed,[28] the reference to Isaiah 6.9f. is closer to the Aramaic Targum than to either the Hebrew or the Greek, and the saying itself is in the parallel form of Semitic verse; on the other hand, though we must not say that "mystery" ($\mu\nu\sigma\tau\dot{\eta}\rho\iota\rho\nu$) is a word that can have come only from a Greek origin, it is a word that would be readily understood (or, it may be, misunderstood) in Greek surroundings. As it stands, the saying has affiliations both with Aramaic-speaking and with Greek-speaking circles. (2) The distinction between disciples and those "outside"[29] corresponds to rabbinic ideas and practice; but it also reflects the evangelist's own redaction of the story, for we can hardly think that he wrote as he did in 4.10f. of οἱ περὶ αὐτόν (those around him) and οἱ ἔξω (those outside) without thinking of what he had written in 3.31–5 of those who, though in close human relationship with Jesus, must stand ἔξω (outside) because they treat Jesus as mad, and those who seated περὶ αὐτόν (around him) are hailed as his new family because they do the will of God. (3) The secret of the kingdom of God refers to the eschatological secret of the relation between the obscure and apparently insignificant ministry of Jesus and the future coming of the kingdom of God in power; but it is also related to a theory of the blinding and hardening of Israel akin to that developed by Paul in Romans 9—11.

It is not my intention here to offer a full exposition of Mark 4.10ff. Enough has been said to show that in this short passage

---

[28] Op. cit., p. 77.
[29] The rabbinic word is החיצונים, that is, the heretics; e.g. Megillah 4.8.

a variety of interests have run together, and at least two historical settings have been combined in such a way that though they can be distinguished they cannot be separated by simple literary dissection. This, moreover, is true (in varying degrees) of the gospels as a whole, for it is seldom that we can make such neat distinctions as that between the parable of the Sower and its interpretation. It remains only to add that, as in the *Iliad* contact between two historical contexts is animated by imagination and patriotism, so in the gospels it is controlled by the creative factor of faith. This, however, becomes a meaningful observation only when we understand the meaning of faith, and faith is itself part of each historical context. We cannot say that the context in the life of Jesus was historical, and that the context in the life of the primitive Church was theological (as an earlier generation of New Testament scholarship tended to say). Each context was theological; the question is how the two theologies are related to each other.

We have thus, it may be, made some advance towards understanding how the gospels come to present us with a problem in the complex of historical and interpretative material they contain. The very fact, however, that the gospel tradition constitutes a problem of this kind makes all the more pressing the question why it was preserved. There can, I think, be only one answer to this question; it was preserved because it could not be forgotten. The historic figure of Jesus of Nazareth was of such overwhelming importance that even when men were thinking of Jesus primarily as the heavenly Lord they chose to interpret, to vary, to modify, to supplement the tradition rather than to abandon it altogether in the interests of a purely supernatural figure; hence the fact (which has now been brought out) that the gospel account of Jesus belongs to two separate and distinguishable contexts, that of his ministry, and that of the Church after the resurrection. We must therefore go on to ask what kind of interest was served in the primitive Church by the preservation of traditions concerning Jesus, how the tradition served these interests, and how it was modified in the process. In this investigation, two points of primary importance will be examined in the second and third chapters. The remainder of this chapter will be given to a more general approach.

The fundamental assertion of the Pauline letters is given in the words, "Jesus is Lord" (Rom. 10.9; 1 Cor. 12.3); Acts (e.g. 2.36), and other parts of the New Testament, bear witness to the same conviction: "He has on his garment and on his thigh a name written, King of kings and Lord of lords" (Rev. 19.16). In the proposition, Jesus is Lord, subject and predicate alike are terms capable of immediate apprehension. "Jesus" is a term intelligible to me because it is the name of a person comparable with myself, in the sense that this person also inhabits a particular area of space and time, and has distinguishable personal characteristics. He is one whom (given suitable circumstances) *I* may encounter as *thou*. This sort of encounter takes place among contemporaries in the category of the personal; among those who are not contemporaries it takes place in the realm of history, history being understood as experienced history.[30] There is a directness about this kind of relationship which requires no explanation because it is one of the fundamental constituents of life, without which life simply would not be what we know it to be. I do not mean that the category of personal encounter is incapable of philosophical analysis, but that this possibility does not destroy its essential simplicity or primitiveness. We all know what it is to meet persons, such as Smith, or Brown, or Jesus of Nazareth.

"Lord" also is a term capable of immediate comprehension. It is useful to theologians to be aware of the use of κύριος (lord) in the Greek Old Testament as the equivalent of the divine name, and of the "lords many" in the hellenistic world; all such knowledge is relevant to New Testament studies. But the word "lord" is complete in itself, and meaningful apart from any background in the history of religions. A κύριος is the owner and master of δοῦλοι, a *dominus* of *servi*, a lord of serfs or slaves; that is, a lord is for me one who has absolute authority over my

---

[30] *Geschichte*, to use the convenient German word.

person. Here too is something which belongs to a category we can undoubtedly understand, even though we may resent it. If I must label this category, I shall, with some hesitation, call it existential. I use the word to denote something that affects me not superficially, not merely intellectually, but in my very being. This takes place in two ways: (1) A lord questions me radically; he has the right to interrogate, and does interrogate, not only what I have done but what I am. My whole existence comes under examination. (2) A lord directs me. I may rebel against his orders, but by definition he has the right to give them, and if I disobey them I not only expose myself to unpleasant consequences, but contradict the meaning of my existence. Thus the effect of a lord is to throw my life into radical existential disturbance, and to give it a new orientation. This happens, however, because, positively, the lord assumes responsibility for my existence, and is therefore to be trusted as well as to be obeyed.

Paul asserts (and in doing so makes no claim to originality—quite the reverse) that Jesus, whose human and historic reality he accepts though he says little about it, is Lord. This at first sight preposterous assertion he justifies by two further claims: (1) that Jesus was the incarnation of a divine person who in distant ages had been God's agent in the work of creation; (2) that in Jesus there had taken place a divine act of redemption (e.g. Rom. 3.24) by which men were redeemed, delivered, and restored to their original relation with God. If these claims are true, then he who is creator and redeemer may without question call upon the faith and obedience of mankind. In a word, Jesus is Lord.

The exposition of the divine act of redemption, and of the meaning of faith and obedience, occupied the whole of Paul's energies. His contribution was, and remains, of fundamental and indispensable importance; yet it leaves out one question, which must be answered if the origins of Christian doctrine, and the significance of Jesus himself, are to be understood. How did this man come to be this lord? How do we pass from the historical to the existential? The Pauline epistles leave the impression that we might step at once from the moment when Jesus was born of a woman, born under the law (Gal. 4.4), to the day on which he died for our sins according to the Scriptures (1 Cor. 15.3), or at least to the night in which he was betrayed (1 Cor. 11.23). This impression is given strongly by the Christological hymn in Philippians 2, and the next chapter of this epistle makes the position intelligible.[31] Paul became a Christian through the direct intervention of the heavenly Christ, whom he immediately recognized as lord (cf. Acts 9.5). His encounter with Jesus was direct, and was not mediated through the record of the historical figure. But we, unlike Paul, are in no position to dispense with the record in the gospels, apart from which we have no knowledge of the person, Jesus, to whom the epithet "Lord" is applied. Is it credible that this historical person should be Lord? Or, to put the question differently, what contribution do the gospels (and the tradition which appears to underlie them) make to the establishing and elucidation of the proposition, Jesus is Lord?

The early creeds interpose two terms between the name Jesus and the title "Lord": they speak of "Jesus Christ his only Son our Lord". It is as Christ and Son of God that Jesus is Lord. This line of thought is at least as early as John 20.31, "These things are written that you may believe that Jesus is the Christ the Son of God, and that believing you may have life in his name", and may be as early as Mark 1.1, if we can accept the longer text: "The beginning of the Gospel of Jesus Christ the Son of God." Even if the concluding words (υἱοῦ (τοῦ) θεοῦ—Son of God) are omitted Mark is very little removed from John because he almost immediately goes on to record the baptism of Jesus, in which Jesus is addressed by God as his Son (1.11). Jesus is the Messiah; he is the Son of God; as such he is the Lord. But this double proposition raises serious historical difficulties. Consider first the claim that Jesus was the Messiah.

There is no doubt that all the synoptic writers believed that Jesus was the Christ. In one of the infancy narratives χριστός

---

[31] See especially Phil. 3.12: "I was overtaken by Christ Jesus."

(Christ) and κύριος (Lord) stand side by side (Luke 2.11) in a combination that recalls the rabbinic "King Messiah"[32] (cf. Mark 15.32; Luke 23.2), and the title "Christ" recurs at important points in the gospel record. The demons, with their supernatural knowledge, know that Jesus is Christ (e.g. Luke 4.41); Peter makes the confession of faith, "Thou art the Christ" (Mark 8.29); the high priest asks Jesus, "Are you the Christ, the Son of the Blessed One?" and (according to Mark) Jesus answers with a direct affirmation (Mark 14.61f.). Such passages as these prove beyond question that the narrators themselves believed that Jesus was the Christ; and we know, from Paul's unquestioning use of the double name Jesus Christ, that the conviction went back far beyond their time: the evangelists did not themselves invent the identification. But how far back does the conviction go? Did Jesus himself believe that he was in his ministry acting as the long-expected Messiah? The question is not a new one,[33] and a very brief sketch of the evidence will suffice.

A number of passages are manifestly editorial and call for no further consideration: Mark 1.1; Matthew 1.1,16,17,18; 11.2 (cf. Luke 7.18); 16.20 (cf. Mark 8.30), 21; 22.42 (cf. Mark 12.35); 24.5 (cf. Mark 13.6); 26.68 (cf. Mark 14.65); 27.17,22 (cf. Mark 15.9,12); Luke 2.26; 4.41 (cf. Mark 1.34); 23.2 (cf. Mark 15.1). These passages show the natural influence of current, unquestioned belief, which the evangelists shared with their contemporaries. There are others which for various reasons do not bear seriously on the historical inquiry into the earliest tradition and the belief of Jesus himself: Mark 9.41 (cf. Matt. 10.42); 13.21 (=Matt. 24.23); Matthew 2.4; 23.10; Luke 2.11; 3.15; 23.39; 24.26,46. There is now little material left—surprisingly little if in fact Jesus did represent himself as Messiah, and was understood to do so. What is left, however, is

---

[32] It has been conjectured that the original text of Luke 2.11 was χριστὸς κυρίου; cf. 2.26 and Psalms of Solomon 17.32. There is very slight MS. support for the conjecture.

[33] For an account of the problem see e.g. F. Hahn, *Christologische Hoheitstitel*, 1964, pp. 133–241.

of considerable importance, and must be considered point by point.

Peter's Confession: Matthew 16.16; Mark 8.29; Luke 9.20. The disciples are asked whom they take Jesus to be. Peter replies, "You are the Christ". If the whole paragraph is read it appears that Jesus neither accepts nor refuses this identification of himself with the Messiah, but goes on to speak in terms of the Son of man. It may be said that the blessing pronounced on Peter in Matthew 16.17 implies that Peter's confession was correct. This was certainly Matthew's view; whether it was also the view of the earlier tradition is open to question. Peter is not congratulated but fiercely attacked in Mark 8.33. This is scarcely consistent with the high praise of Peter recorded by Matthew, which, if it is historical at all, may well belong to a post-resurrection setting, though such a setting also would raise difficulties of its own.[34] The confession thus cannot be taken as evidence of what Jesus himself thought of his own person and work; it is nevertheless important and must not be simply dismissed. We shall see that it is not inconsistent with a quantity of other material in the gospels whose historical position seems reasonably secure, though we must not conclude that it is an adequate or satisfactory expression of this material, which raises the question of messiahship.

David's son and David's lord: Matthew 22.41–5; Mark 12.35ff.; Luke 20.41–4. Interpretations of this passage have on the whole followed two lines. (1) Jesus is arguing that descent from David is not necessary to messiahship. It is implied that he himself is not descended from David (as the Matthaean and Lucan genealogies, and other passages, affirm), but may nevertheless claim to be Messiah, since Psalm 110.1 proves that the Messiah is David's Lord rather than his descendant. Alternatively, (2) Jesus is spiritualizing the idea of messiahship. The Messiah (as he understands the term) is not to be simply a "bigger and better" David, a more successful soldier and more prosperous king. He is to be of spiritual origin and supernatural

---

[34] O. Cullmann, *Peter: Disciple—Apostle—Martyr*, 1953, p. 183, places the saying within the passion narrative.

authority. The objection to both these interpretations is that they assume that Jesus was openly claiming to be Messiah—a non-Davidic or spiritual Messiah perhaps; whereas it is manifest from an analysis of the rest of the gospel material that he made no such claim. The saying may be a veiled presentation of messiahship;[35] or perhaps a throwing back of a popular Christian proof text into the tradition. It should be compared with Mark 9.11ff., where another commonly accepted scribal proposition is discussed: "Why do the scribes say that Elijah must come first?" Mark's answer is twofold: (a) the proposition is in fact true, and has already been fulfilled; (b) though true, the proposition is incomplete, because it omits the Scriptural truth that both the returning Elijah, and the Son of man, must suffer. This overlooked factor has meant that the fulfilment of the scribal hope, though genuine, has necessarily been unobserved. It is probable that Mark understood the scribal proposition discussed in 12.35ff. on similar lines. On the one hand it is true, and in process of fulfilment—the Davidic Messiah is present; on the other, it is incomplete, for it ignores the scriptural truth that the Messiah is David's Lord, and is thus different from David. Hence the messiahship, though real, is necessarily unobserved. If taken in this way the paragraph fits into one of Mark's central themes, and probably into the context of dispute about messiahship conducted between Church and Synagogue rather than in the life of Jesus himself, though the latter possibility is not completely excluded.[36]

Only one passage with explicit reference to messiahship remains—the high priest's question (Matt. 26.63f.; Mark 14.61f.; Luke 22.67–70). It is only in Mark that Jesus answers with the explicit words, "I am"; but the context shows that the less clear expressions used by Matthew and Luke amount

---

[35] "It half conceals and half reveals the 'Messianic Secret'", V. Taylor, *The Gospel according to St Mark*, 1952, p. 493.

[36] If the saying is authentic we should probably think of it as a reply to accusations, based on quasi-messianic activity of Jesus (see pp. 23f.), that he was claiming messiahship.

to affirmations.[37] Jesus affirms that he is the Messiah and Son of God at precisely the moment at which it is inconceivable that anyone should believe him. This affirmation is indispensable to the development of the Passion Story, in which Jesus suffers as the King of the Jews. This theme must be taken up in the second chapter; here it must be sufficient to note that material such as this, located within the story of the trial, can scarcely be taken as evidence for the public teaching of Jesus, though it may well be evidence for questions that may have been genuinely raised by the actions rather than the words of Jesus.

Finally we should note the story of the entry of Jesus into Jerusalem (Matt. 21.1-9; Mark 11.1-10; Luke 19.28-40). Here it is easy to trace the progressive interpretation of the incident in messianic terms; but even Matthew, who with his quotation of Zechariah 9.9 and reference to two beasts is particularly explicit, states only (21.11) that the crowds saw in Jesus a messianic prophet, not the Messiah himself, and though the primary Marcan narrative bears witness to messianic excitement it does not suggest that Jesus was making a public claim that he was himself the Messiah.

I do not see how the gospel material, critically evaluated, can lead to the conclusion that Jesus publicly stated the claim, "I am the Messiah"; or even that he thought privately in these terms—though it is well to make quite clear that though we have some evidence on the basis of which we can discuss what Jesus *said* we have no additional evidence that might tell us what he thought but did not say. This however is not the whole truth. The ministry of Jesus formed a battle-ground on which was fought out a struggle for the leadership of Judaism.[38] It is impossible that such a struggle should not have involved messianic ideas; that is, even if Jesus did not himself intend to raise the issue of messiahship it will almost certainly have been

[37] In Matthew (26.64) Jesus replies, "You have said so"; in Luke (22.70), "You say that I am"; but the high priest assumes that Jesus has admitted the charge: Matt. 26.65; Luke 22.71.

[38] Cf. E. Schweizer, *Church Order in the New Testament*, 1961, 2d.

raised by others as a result of his actions. This seems in fact to have occurred; and there were elements in the teaching and work of Jesus that led directly to it. Some of these I shall consider later, but it is already easy to see how the tradition worked. A theme implicit rather than explicit in the underlying history, but of great importance in the earliest days of the Church, was worked up and developed in such a way as to represent concretely the lordship of Jesus. The process was a risky one, because the proposition "Jesus is the Christ" involves at the same time less and more than the proposition "Jesus is Lord". It takes us out of the realms of the personal and existential and into that of history, understood now not as experienced history but as recorded and studied history,[39] for it is impossible to understand "Christ" (as it is possible to understand "Jesus" and "Lord") on the basis of common human experience. The word is meaningful only to those who have learnt something of post-biblical Judaism. This means further that a nationalist element is inherent in the word, an element which had to be dealt with either by theological interpretation (as in the fourth gospel), or by the simpler expedient of transforming the title in question (Christ) into a proper name (as happened elsewhere in the early Church).[40]

The second term introduced in the creeds to ease the passage from Jesus to Lord is "Son of God". As with Messiah, we may say without hesitation that the evangelists believed that Jesus was the Son of God, and that this conviction was current in the tradition for some time before the gospels were written. Even if Mark 1.1 is excluded, this gospel provides adequate evidence for its author's view: 1.11; 3.11; 5.7; 9.7; (12.6); 13.32; 14.61; 15.39. Many of these passages are taken over in Matthew and Luke, who also provide additional material, in the birth narratives (Matt. 2.15; Luke 1.32,35), and elsewhere, mainly in editorial modifications of Mark (Matt. 14.33; 16.16; 27.40,43). There is also the evidently late baptismal formula of Matthew 28.19. In addition, there are two important Q passages: in the

[39] *Historie*; cf. n. 27.
[40] See further p. 66.

temptation narrative (Matt. 4.3,6; Luke 4.3,9), and in the
great thanksgiving (Matt. 11.27; Luke 10.22).

Most of this material falls out of consideration immediately
so far as the public proclamation of Jesus is concerned. This is
true of the words spoken at the Baptism and Transfiguration
(whatever the historical basis of these stories may be), and of
passages in the infancy narratives. The Q Temptation should
probably be regarded as a theological interpretation (in terms
of biblical debate) of the more primitive Marcan story; in any
case, it makes no claim to represent what Jesus publicly said
about himself. In Mark 14.61 (it is instructive to note how this
is modified in Luke) the term Son of God appears along with
Christ, and should be understood as a supplementary messianic
title. The kings of Israel had always been sons of God, and
naturally this would be pre-eminently true of the messianic
king. Little is left by way of explicit statement but Mark 13.32
and the Q saying of Matthew 11.27 = Luke 10.22.

Discussion of the genuineness of Mark 13.32 has by no means
reached an agreed conclusion. Since Dalman's time it has been
fairly widely recognized that "the Son" and "the Father"
"appear as a ready-made formula, and are therefore to be
attributed to the influence of the Church vocabulary on the
text",[41] and Bousset[42] suggested that the verse was made up in
order to deal with the problem caused by the delay of the
parousia. Those who defend the verse often recall Schmiedel's
observation that no Christian would have made up a verse that
alleged the ignorance of Jesus; Dr Taylor[43] sums up: "Its
offence seals its genuineness". There is force in this argument,
but it seems to have been overlooked that it can defend at most
the substance, and in no way the formulation, of the verse.
Even if the substance of the verse is genuine (and it seems to me
very doubtful whether it can be regarded as consistent with the
teaching of Jesus as a whole), the description of Jesus by the
most honorific title available would be precisely the sort of

[41] G. Dalman, *The Words of Jesus*, 1909, p. 194.
[42] W. Bousset, *Kyrios Christos*, 1926, pp. 43f., 52.
[43] Op. cit., p. 522, giving also the reference to Schmiedel.

compensation that tradition would introduce. If Jesus is to confess an ignorance to which he has voluntarily submitted during the conditions of his incarnate life, tradition will see that in doing so he is recognized in the conditions of his pre-incarnate life, as the Son, the equally divine correlative of the Father. It would thus be unwise to build on Mark 13.32 in a reconstruction of the teaching, or even of the thought, of Jesus.

In both Matthew and Luke the Q saying about Father and Son (Matt. 11.27 = Luke 10.22) is handed down in a context in which it is introduced by the doom of the Galilean cities, which have not repented at a preaching that would have moved even Tyre and Sidon. The saying about Father and Son provides the positive counterpart, and at the same time the explanation, of the condemnatory saying. The ministry of Jesus is paradoxical in its effects. It is understood not by the wise, but by babes; that is, by disciples who, though without rabbinic training, are prepared to accept the kingdom with the simplicity of children. Interpretation of the saying will thus naturally proceed from the last clause: revelation of the Father is through the Son, and if the Son is rejected, if Jesus' preaching is not heeded, there is no revelation and no hope: hence the condemnation of Bethsaida, Chorazin, and Capernaum. This failure of recognition is moreover natural and humanly speaking inevitable, since the Son is known only to the Father. There is nothing in the appearance of Jesus to demonstrate his authority, and only a revelation from the Father (cf. Matt. 16.17) can disclose his identity: hence the failure of Bethsaida, Chorazin, and Capernaum. This is the force also of Matthew 11.25 = Luke 10.21 (cf. Mark 4.11). We have here a theme which runs very deep into the gospel tradition, and a conviction (that there are no outward signs to guarantee the identification of Jesus) which is contrary to the line of development which the tradition as a whole shows. We are therefore dealing here with material that has in essence a strong claim to historical trustworthiness; but it is placed in a setting for which no such claim can be made, and it follows that the wording (as distinct from the substance) of the verse may well be secondary; that is, the neat Father-Son formulation cannot be confidently traced back to Jesus.

To these passages which refer explicitly to Jesus as the Son should be added the parable of Mark 12.1–12. If this is read as it stands there can be little doubt that the one beloved son sent by the owner of the vineyard at the end of a series of slaves represents Jesus as the Son of God. I shall not here review all the arguments that have been used in support of the view that this allegorical feature is secondary, or the replies that have been made to them. It ought not to be dismissed merely because it is allegorical.[44] A Jew could not tell a story about a vineyard without embarking upon allegory (cf. Isa. 5.7). But the paragraph as it stands bears undoubted marks of compilation. V.9 ("he will come and destroy those husbandmen") is taken up by v. 12 ("they perceived that he had spoken this parable against them"), and the quotation from Psalm 118.22 has no point of contact in the parable itself,[45] which says nothing of the vindication of the murdered son but speaks only of the punishment of his murderers. Moreover, the parable interrupts what is evidently a sequence of questions, and thus probably owes its place to Mark's editorial hand. It helps to answer the question of 11.28 (What is the source of Jesus' authority?) and it leads to the pronouncement of 12.17: as tribute must be paid to Caesar, so God's due must be given to him—he requires his share of the fruit of the vineyard. These considerations suggest that in 12.1–12 we have before us a sharpened Christological form of a parable which may originally in simpler terms have emphasized that the present was the time of God's decisive claim upon his people, and that the judgement of Israel had now begun.

It would be a mistake to suppose that this observation robs the parable of its significance, even of its Christological significance. It takes away from it nothing but a certain amount of allusive technical vocabulary, and leaves unimpaired the

[44] See C. E. B. Cranfield, *The Gospel according to St Mark*, 1963, pp. 366ff.
[45] The use of Ps. 118.22 may well have begun after the resurrection (cf. Acts 4.11; 1 Pet. 2.7), and been read back into the gospels.

conviction that the mission of Jesus marks the climax of God's dealings with his people: this is God's last demand for the fruit that Israel ought to produce, and a demand which God proposes to back to the limit by vindicating the rejected messenger and punishing those who reject him. On any showing, Jesus is related to the prophets, but greater than they. This passage therefore will stand with those that were referred to above, passages which, though they do not use the technical language of messiahship, show Jesus claiming leadership within the people of God, and therefore invite interpretation in messianic terms. At this point, after our discussion of passages referring to Jesus as "the Son", we should note also his conviction that God was his father. Whether or not Jesus thought the fatherhood to be unique in kind, the conviction was unique; for though Mark 14.36, with the Gethsemane narrative as a whole, raises historical problems, [46] we can hardly doubt that the unique Aramaic *Abba* goes back to Jesus himself. [47]

Jesus refused to define the authority with which he spoke and acted. The explicit rejection in Mark 11.33 of any attempt to state its source simply confirms his refusal to make use—at the very least, to make public use—of messianic or similar categories. Nevertheless, he acted with authority. [48] The question of Mark 11.28 is perhaps better evidence for this than 1.22,27, which, as they stand, are no doubt editorial formulations, though they serve to crystallize the impression made by the gospel material as a whole. This impression was made not only on the friends but also on the enemies of Jesus, who could not deny, though they might explain away, his ability to cast out demons. This practical manifestation of authority (expressed also in teaching and in personal relations) pointed to a unique connection between Jesus and the kingdom of God: "If I by the finger of God cast out demons, then is the kingdom of God come upon you" (Luke 11.20). Jesus announced the near

---

[46] See below, pp. 46ff.

[47] For the significance of *Abba* see J. Jeremias, *The Central Message of the New Testament*, 1965, pp. 17–30; and *Abba*, 1966, pp. 15–67.

[48] This point is emphasized by G. Bornkamm, *Jesus of Nazareth*, 1960.

approach of the kingdom (e.g. Mark 1.15); he did this, how-ever, not as a detached observer, but as one with whom the kingdom itself was bound up. Blessed were those who saw and heard the things he did and said; but for those who witnessed them and still did not repent a sterner fate was in store than that of Sodom and Gomorrah. Most important of all (when we have regard to the Jewish situation in which his ministry was cast) is the fact that he challenged and himself replaced the Torah. He claimed no rabbinic authority (Mark 11.27–33 again), yet he took it on himself to issue new *halakoth*, of binding authority; and where Torah had failed to create a relationship between man and God, he made a new one, by his search for the outcast and sinful, and by his exercise of forgiveness. It is in this framework of absolute authority that we must under-stand his summons to an odd variety of ignorant and irreligious men, and their response to it. Follow me, he said; and they obeyed.

The gospels thus, on analysis, present us with a paradoxical and disorderly situation. They show us Jesus acting as Lord; so far, they justify the faith of the Church expressed in the words, "Jesus is Lord". He who is now the Lord in heaven, attested as such by the resurrection, anticipated his present dominion by the miraculous and magisterial authority with which he acted during his earthly ministry. The tradition, and in due course the evangelists, went on to assert that Jesus had this authority because he was the Messiah and uniquely the Son of God. Historical analysis suggests that Jesus claimed neither of these roles; by asserting them, the tradition was trying to prove the right thing in the wrong way. In the wrong way: yet these first steps in Christological thought were inevitable, and in the end not mistaken. We must ask, however, whether it is not possible to find more convincing historical roots for the lordship of Jesus. Three may be mentioned, two of them very briefly because they have already been discussed.

1. Jesus was aware, in a peculiarly intense and intimate way, that God was his father. The intensity and intimacy of his

religious life are attested not only by the accounts of his prayers but also by his quiet assumption that what he says expresses fully and authoritatively the will of God. Mark 11.27–33 has positive as well as negative significance, for Jesus, when he refuses a direct answer to the inquiry about the source of his authority, nevertheless implies quite clearly that it comes from God. The refusal of a definition of his authority arises out of the fact that a definition would limit and diminish it. Jesus, then, was aware of God as his father. How then could he be other than God's Son? And, since Son of God was primarily a messianic title, how could he not be the Messiah? It is easy to trace, and up to a point to justify, the course taken by the tradition as it was handed down and interpreted; but, in defining, it ran at each stage the grave risk of damaging rather than securing Jesus' authority.

2. There is a close connection between the person and work of Jesus and the kingdom of God. It will suffice for illustration if at this point I simply refer back to what I said earlier about Mark 4.10ff. The "secret of the kingdom of God" is, as the various agricultural parables show, the mysterious relation between the obscure and repressed activity of Jesus and the future coming of the kingdom in glory and power. This is as inexplicable, but as real, as the relation between the process of sowing and the harvest.[49] This is not to say that the kingdom is present, certainly not that it is present in its fullness, nor is it to say that Jesus is, or even that he will be, the messianic king. It was, however, easy to draw this conclusion, and we see a further point of departure for the messianic interpretation of Jesus which developed in the tradition.

3. Examination of almost all the titles ascribed to Jesus in the gospels leads to the conclusion that they arose in the course of the tradition, or at least that they were not used or accepted by him, though some of them may have been used of him (or against him) by his contemporaries. The most notable exception

---

[49] See N. A. Dahl, "The Parables of Growth" in *Studia Theologica V*, 1952, pp. 132–66, especially 140–7.

is the term "Son of man". It is true that in recent years a number of attempts have been made to show that this term also is a contribution made by the Church to the tradition, but none of them seems to me to have dealt adequately with the fact that "Son of man", so common a term in the gospels, occurs only once in the rest of the New Testament.[50] The fact that the expectation of the kingdom of God (which we can hardly doubt belongs to the preaching of Jesus himself) and the expectation of the coming of the Son of man form in the tradition two separate layers which are not connected with each other[51] is offset by another fact, that what is said about the kingdom is closely parallel to what is said about the Son of man. Each is present in obscurity and humiliation (though not without some secret anticipated effectiveness and authority), and each will come in manifest glory and power. If this parallelism had been the work of the Church the two terms would have appeared together, as Dr Vielhauer has shown that they do not. As it is, the parallelism constitutes a strong argument that both kingdom of God and Son of man belong to the earliest strata of the tradition.

To say this is not to say that every occurrence of "Son of man" should be regarded as coming from the lips of Jesus. Dr Schweizer[52] has analysed the whole of the material and reached a conclusion that he himself described as surprising. "Even if in matters of detail some questions remain, it is nevertheless apparent that, taken as a whole, the *parousia*-sayings are the most insecure, and those that denote the earthly Jesus the most secure."[53] The conclusion is not only surprising but unconvincing. It is impossible here to follow Dr Schweizer through the whole list of passages, and I must be content for

---

[50] We must here leave open the possibility, argued recently by A. J. B. Higgins (*Jesus and the Son of Man*, 1964), that Jesus spoke of the Son of man as a person other than himself.

[51] See P. Vielhauer, "Gottesreich und Menschensohn in der Verkündigung Jesu" in *Festschrift für Günther Dehn*, 1957, pp. 51–79.

[52] E. Schweizer, "Der Menschensohn" in *Zeitschrift für die neutestamentliche Wissenschaft* 50, 1959, pp. 185–209; also "The Son of Man Again" in *New Testament Studies* 9, 1963, pp. 256–61.

[53] *Zeitschrift für die neutestamentliche Wissenschaft*, 50, 1959, pp. 200f.

the most part with generalizations. The strongest general arguments in support of the apocalyptic Son of man passages are that they have a readily ascertainable setting in the Judaism with which, we may suppose, Jesus was familiar, and that in them Jesus appears to speak of a person other than himself. "Whosoever shall be ashamed of me and of my words in this adulterous and sinful generation, the Son of man shall be ashamed of him, when he comes in the glory of his Father with the holy angels" (Mark 8.38). This is however a verse of crucial importance,[54] for it cuts across the trichotomy that is usually imposed upon the Son of man material. It is true that much of this can be divided into sets dealing with (*a*) the future glorious coming of the Son of man, (*b*) his death and resurrection, and (*c*) his earthly ministry. But Mark 8.38 combines these elements (though not all under the term "Son of man"). That men may possibly be ashamed of Jesus and his words implies his teaching ministry, with the rejection of his words by those authorities who might be supposed to be in a position to judge their truth; and that he himself will be placed in a position of obloquy, disgrace, and, we may reasonably add, suffering—suffering such as a few verses earlier is predicted for him under the title of Son of man. It is men's attitude to the rejected teaching and despised person of Jesus that will determine the attitude to them of the glorious Son of man. If we are to see a theologizing influence at work on the tradition it is most probably to be found in the passages that depict the ministry of Jesus on earth as already that of the Son of man; yet Dr Schweizer has made a strong case for regarding precisely these as authentic.

The exact sense of the term Son of man, and the extent of its use by Jesus, must await discussion in later lectures. Its importance at the moment is that it can reasonably be viewed as a connecting thread which holds together Jesus' work in the present and in the future. Even if he did not explicitly assert his own personal identity with the Son of man of the future, he did

---

[54] For further discussion, see below, pp. 79ff.

claim that the future was in the hands of the Son of man, and that it was organically related to his own words and deeds in the present. Here too, later tradition found a means of systematizing the historical tradition about Jesus in terms of the theological view of his importance, for in both Judaism and Christianity there was a progressive identification of the Son of man with the Messiah. But if Jesus did speak of himself as Son of man, it cannot have been in such a way as to create the impression that the Son of man was the Messiah. As Son of man, he represented humanity in the process of recovering the lordship for which man was created (Ps. 8). This he did by living out the subordination of which the Psalm speaks, and achieving the lost destiny of man in complete obedience to his Creator.[55] This obedience was the way back to rightful dominion, and it was therefore of the essence of the Son of man's work that he should serve rather than be served.[56] Hence Jesus taught his disciples to recognize humility and service as the only marks of greatness. Here was the sense in which Jesus understood himself to be the Lord.

What I have said so far amounts to a radical criticism of the Church's handling of the historical tradition about Jesus. He himself had sought no labels, no categories by which to express his lordship within and over the human race. Secure in his knowledge of, trust in, and obedience to the Father, he had pursued his way with the authority God had given him, so that those who knew him best, even before the resurrection sealed and universalized the matter, had recognized him as Lord. But this story of a lord incognito had seemed hardly to bear the weight that was laid upon it, and as it was handed on Jesus was more and more fitted into the niches of accepted greatness (such as messiahship), and it was seldom observed that this was contrary to his own practice, and could easily have been derogatory to his own greatness.

The tradition invites and deserves this criticism. Yet it is only

---

[55] This point will be taken up again; see pp. 95ff.
[56] In the apocalyptic development of the Son of man figure this truth was lost sight of.

just to add that what was done was inevitable, and in its own way right. The early tradition contained messianic hints, which called for development, and it would have been impossible to argue the place of Jesus in Judaism without introducing (if it was not there to begin with) the category of messiahship, and with it that of adoptive sonship. Because the tradition was a genuine historical tradition, dealing with the real life of Jesus in his Jewish environment, it was necessary to argue the place of Jesus in Judaism. Thus the historical tradition was obliged to go beyond history, sometimes even to falsify history, precisely because it was historical. This fact constitutes the problem of the historical Jesus; at the same time it contains the only solution of the problem that we are likely to find. The second and third lectures lead us to consider special aspects of this problem.

2

Christ Crucified

———◆◆◆◆———

Did Jesus predict that he would have to suffer and die? The gospels relate that he did so. In Mark 8.31 he declares that the Son of man must suffer many things, and whatever the term Son of man may mean elsewhere, here the amplification of the bare prediction that follows ("He must be rejected by the elders and the chief priests and the scribes, and be killed"), and the further amplifications of later but similar predictions, especially in Mark 10.33f. ("The Son of man shall be betrayed to the chief priests and the scribes, and they shall condemn him to death and hand him over to the Gentiles, and they shall mock him and spit on him and scourge him and kill him"), prove beyond any doubt that the Son of man is Jesus, and that the evangelists at least understood Jesus himself to have foretold his passion and to have predicted it in some detail.

These gospel predictions have, however, often been taken as sham predictions, predictions made after the event. Jesus did not, in truth, foretell his coming suffering, but Christians, handing down the tradition of his life and teaching, felt it intolerable that he should have been surprised by his fate, and accordingly wrote predictions of it into the tradition. "Can any doubt exist that they are all *vaticinia ex eventu*?"[1]

[1] R. Bultmann, *Theologie des Neuen Testaments*, 1948–53, p. 30.

This is not an opinion to be lightly dismissed, though it needs to be carefully stated. Wellhausen[2] argues as follows.

> The idea of a suffering Messiah was not prepared for by the prophecies of the Old Testament; no one can get this idea out of them who does not bring it with him and put it in. There thus takes place a tremendous leap from the proper Messiah to another, who shared with him only his name, and was in fact no Messiah at all. And this leap cannot be understood *a priori*, but only *post factum*.

What Wellhausen overlooks in this otherwise convincing argument is that Mark 8.31, and the other predictions, do not say that the Messiah will suffer. They say that the Son of man will suffer; and this is not the same thing. It may in the end prove to be no more intelligible, but that is a matter that will have to be considered later. We have already seen that Jesus did not proclaim himself as Messiah, so that the presupposition of Wellhausen's case, as he states it, falls away; though this is not to say that the case could not be more carefully stated in such a way that it would not be open to exception.

To the view that the predictions of the passion were *ex post facto* prophecies it has often been objected that they can be understood on a purely human level and therefore make no impossible demands on the reader's credulity.

> How should it have been otherwise? [Jesus] must have had a clear impression of the irreconcilable enmity of his adversaries, and he could observe the untrustworthiness and capriciousness of the people every day. Since his whole activity ran counter to the endeavours of the scribes and the favourite ideas of the people, sooner or later there had to be a collision.[3]

This objection, taken alone, has genuine historical validity, for, historically speaking, there is nothing more certain in the story of Jesus than that he provoked the fiercest opposition on the part of some at least of the authorities of his people, so that, unless

[2] J. Wellhausen, *Einleitung in die drei ersten Evangelien*, 1905, p. 91. Wellhausen—perhaps unnecessarily—allows Isa. 52.13—53.12 as an exception, but this does not affect the position in the gospels.

[3] J. Weiss, in *Die Schriften des Neuen Testaments*, 3rd edn, by W. Bousset and W. Heitmüller, 1917, i, p. 149.

he was prepared to withdraw, a head-on clash was likely to result. In itself, however, it is by no means an adequate treatment of the question, for so far as the material is capable of such simple matter-of-fact treatment it is irrelevant to the purposes of the evangelists and the story they had to tell. It was not their intention to give an account of an irreconcilable quarrel which resulted in the death of one of the participants, but to assert a theological truth, for the necessity (δεῖ) of the suffering and death of Jesus was not a contingent but an absolute and divine necessity.[4] Mark 8.31 claims that Jesus must die, not because it was impossible to patch up the quarrel between him and the Jewish officials but because this was what God had determined as the destiny of the Son of man and the means by which mankind was to be restored.

This is the point we may learn from Wrede's dry comment on the attempt to salvage some kernel of historical truth from the passion predictions.

> In any case, if it would be bold to assert that Jesus can never before the final days have expressed presentiments of suffering and even of death, it is certainly extremely difficult to conceive that, from a long way off, he arrived at a real certainty of death, at a messianic[5] evaluation of it, at a point where the thought became so powerful that it filled his whole consciousness.[6]

We have achieved nothing of note if we have merely abstracted from the predictions the conclusion that Jesus may have had some inkling of his fate before it overtook him.

The connection of thought established by Wrede seems to me correct; but he has not followed it out in the right direction. It is true that a mere forecast that the conflict with Judaism would become more and more embittered, and come to a violent climax, would be of no significance. Yet it is also true, as Wrede allows, that there is no reason why Jesus should not

---

[4] See, for example, E. Fascher, "Theologische Beobachtungen zu δεῖ" in *Neutestamentliche Studien für Rudolf Bultmann* (*Beihefte zur Zeitschrift für die neutestamentliche Wissenschaft* 21, 1954), pp. 228–54.

[5] Cf. the point made above (p. 36) with reference to the quotation from Wellhausen.

[6] W. Wrede, *Das Messiasgeheimnis in den Evangelien*, 1963, p. 88.

have made such a forecast; only (we may continue), as a reasonable man (to say no more) he cannot have left the matter, and the forecast, there. We cannot imagine that he would say: "It is clear that, if I pursue my present course, my adversaries will attempt to put me out of the way. Indeed, I fear they will succeed in doing this, and so my proclamation of the kingdom will come to an end, and we shall all be back where we were when I began my ministry." If Jesus had nothing better to say than this he would presumably have withdrawn, recognizing the argument of *force majeure*. This conclusion he must have drawn, however, unless he was able not only to foretell his death but also to interpret it in the same eschatological context in which he interpreted his ministry as a whole.[7] We thus reach the conclusion that if Jesus predicted his death (and there is no reason why he should not have done so), he also interpreted it. This conclusion does not carry with it as a corollary that all the predictions and interpretations found in the gospels are authentic utterances of Jesus; on the contrary, every one of them calls for detailed critical examination, and some of them show very clear signs of later construction; but at least there is no *a priori* reason why every one of them should be dismissed from historical discussion, and we may reasonably begin an inquiry into Jesus' own understanding of the experience of suffering which he knew was approaching—so far as this understanding is reflected in the earliest levels of the tradition. It may be that the question posed at the beginning of this chapter is not to be answered with a simple monosyllable.

As we set about this inquiry it will be worth while first to develop a point made negatively in the criticism of Wellhausen. Wellhausen is quite right in saying that the only way to get a suffering Messiah out of the Old Testament is first of all to read this idea into the Old Testament.[8] But this observation, though

---

[7] Cf. J. Jeremias in *Theologisches Wörterbuch zum Neuen Testament*, Vol. V, p. 711.

[8] See S. Mowinckel, *He That Cometh*, 1956, especially pp. 327f. Mowinckel's judgement is the more important because he is less likely than most to underestimate the significance in this context of the role of the king in the cultus.

true, is irrelevant to our inquiry. That he must be accepted as the Messiah was no part of Jesus' proclamation, and even in the latest strata of the tradition, in which the messiahship of Jesus is assumed without question, predictions are not given in the form, "The Messiah must suffer". Goguel, approaching the matter from a different angle, and with a number of valuable insights and observations, is nevertheless also mistaken in saying, "Jesus did not believe himself to be the Messiah *although* he had to suffer; he believed that he was the Messiah *because* he had to suffer. This is the great paradox, the great originality of his Gospel".[9] This paradox, that of a suffering Messiah, is one that the gospels do not make. Rather, they go out of their way to avoid it. The dropping of the word "Christ", between Mark 8.29 and 31, and the introduction in its place of "the Son of man", can hardly be accidental. In none of the places, up to the passion narrative itself, in which the word "Christ" is used, is it directly connected with suffering. It is true that, when the moment of suffering actually arrives, in the trials and in the title on the cross itself, Jesus is represented as the Christ, the king of the Jews; but this, an important matter to which we shall attend in due course, has nothing to do with his predictions and interpretations. It may be that Goguel's paradox should be reworded: Jesus, who did not claim to live as the Messiah, died as the Messiah. More of this below.

It is equally true that the sufferings are not interpreted as those of the Servant of the Lord,[10] the figure known to us from a number of passages in Deutero-Isaiah, notably (in this connection) Isaiah 52.13—53.12. In the synoptic gospels there are only two quotations from Isaiah 53. At Matthew 8.17, Isaiah 53.4 is quoted with reference to the healing ministry of Jesus. His own suffering and death are not alluded to at all; and it is surely significant that the words "He took our sicknesses and bore our diseases" can be used without any hint at vicarious

[9] M. Goguel, *The Life of Jesus*, 1933, p. 392.
[10] See M. D. Hooker, *Jesus and the Servant*, 1959; also my "The Background of Mark 10.45" in *New Testament Essays: Studies in Memory of T. W. Manson*, ed. A. J. B. Higgins, 1959, pp. 1–18.

suffering. As late as the final editing of Matthew there were responsible Christians who did not see in the fourth Servant Song any necessary allusion to the passion, but, though they gave the song a Christological interpretation, understood it in a completely different way. The second quotation is at Luke 22.37, where Isaiah 53.12 ("He was counted with sinners") is quoted, rather, it seems, to prepare the disciples for the fate in store for them (see vv. 35f.) than as an explanation of the role in which Jesus himself was to suffer. So far as the verse refers to the immediately following events it points not to suffering and its redemptive efficacy, but to the particular fact that Jesus was to be crucified along with two evil-doers.

To these passages some would add Mark 10.45; 14.24. The former of these I have discussed elsewhere;[11] it contains no direct literary allusion to Isaiah 53. Any contact between Mark 14.24 and Isaiah 53 is even more remote. The word δοῦλος (slave) is never applied to Jesus in the gospels. The word παῖς[12] is used of him twice. In Luke 2.43 it simply describes him as a twelve-year-old boy; this is irrelevant. In Matthew 12.18 it appears in a quotation from Isaiah 42.1. This is indeed important, but we must note that the ancients did not closely associate Isaiah 42 with Isaiah 53—the connection belongs to critical Old Testament scholarship; and that in Matthew this passage (like 8.17, dealt with above) has no connection with the suffering and death of Jesus but only with his beneficent healing ministry (and, in this passage, its concealment). The evidence that has been adduced to show that Jesus regarded himself, or was regarded by the evangelists, as the suffering Servant[13] is unconvincing. Only Matthew appears to have thought of him as the Servant at all, and even he not as the *suffering* Servant. It has been suggested that the voice at the Baptism (Mark 1.11) speaks in terms only of Isaiah 42.1 (and not of Psalm 2.7), and

[11] See n. 10 above.
[12] An ambiguous Greek word, which sometimes means *servant*, sometimes *child*.
[13] See especially the article παῖς θεοῦ by J. Jeremias and W. Zimmerli in *Theologisches Wörterbuch zum Neuen Testament*, Vol. V, pp. 653–713; also O. Cullmann, *Die Christologie des Neuen Testaments*, 1957, pp. 50–81.

that the word υἱός (son) is due not to the use of the Psalm but to misinterpretation of the word παῖς, which originally represented עבד (slave) but was taken in its other sense of "child". But as long as the word υἱός stands in the text this suggestion cannot be more than a guess, and in fact the allusion to Isaiah 42 seems to be the subordinate one. Other passages cannot be discussed in detail here. It is significant that those who use them find themselves obliged to argue sometimes from the Hebrew text of Isaiah, sometimes from the LXX, and sometimes from post-Christian versions. This does not add to the credibility of the arguments.

It would be foolish to assert that Jesus, who evidently knew the Old Testament well, had somehow overlooked Isaiah 53 in his reading of it, or that, for some reason unknown to us, he refused on principle to make any reference to it. It would be even more foolish to suppose that the early Church in its search for Old Testament material bearing on the person and work of Jesus failed to notice the chapter, for we know that some New Testament writers (e.g. the author of 1 Peter) did make use of it. But we can say with confidence that it appears only on the margin of the synoptic tradition, and that no discussion of the teaching of Jesus, or of the teaching of the gospels, can take it as a major constituent of its reconstruction. And to interpret "Son of man" as if this title were simply a cypher for "Servant of the Lord" is methodologically illegitimate. If we cannot interpret the passion material in terms of "Son of man", the title used in almost all the predictions of suffering, and the only title that can be traced back with much credibility to Jesus himself, we shall be obliged to recognize that we cannot interpret the passion at all; or rather, we shall be obliged to recognize (a) that we cannot approach Jesus' own understanding of the significance of his death, and (b) that the synoptic tradition contains no serious thinking on the subject at all.

There is in fact in "Son of man" so good a basis for the understanding of the passion that it is surprising that students have sought one elsewhere. The gospel use of "Son of man", though highly distinctive and perhaps owing something to other sources also, rests primarily upon Daniel 7, where the term[14] makes its first appearance in an eschatological context. The contents of the chapter are too familiar to call for detailed summary. After four horrifying beasts there appears one "like a son of man", that is, a human, not a beast-like, figure. He is brought near to the throne of God, and receives a universal kingdom. It is made clear in the later part of the chapter that this human figure represents the "people of the saints of the Most High" (v.27), that is, Israel;[15] or, more accurately perhaps, faithful Israel, the righteous remnant within Israel.

Now we know the circumstances in which this Son of man oracle was written. The attack on Judaism engineered by Antiochus IV Epiphanes had begun; the little horn of the fourth beast, "in which were eyes like the eyes of a man, and a mouth speaking great things" (7.8), represents Antiochus himself. The Maccabean revolt had scarcely begun; even if it was actually in operation, the author of Daniel did not set his hope upon it: "They shall receive a little help" (11.34). For the people of the saints there was not much to look forward to but suffering. The suffering, however, would not be the end of the story. God himself would intervene to reverse the fortunes of his people, and after their suffering they—represented in the vision by the Son of man figure—would receive the position of authority which the beast had occupied.

The author of this book was too clear-sighted to suppose that all his people were "saints" in the conventional sense of the term. Some had actually proved traitors to the national faith. There was no future for them (e.g. 11.30; 12.2). Moreover, the people as a whole must have been sinful; this was why they had been called upon to suffer. Hence in 9.4–19 Daniel offers a prayer of penitence, acknowledging that the suffering is due to the apostasy of the people. "All Israel has transgressed thy law

---

[14] In the form without articles, בר אנש, υἱὸς ἀνθρώπου.

[15] It does not make much difference as far as the present argument is concerned whether we take "saints" to be explanatory of "people", or think of them as heavenly beings (see M. Noth, "Die Heiligen des Höchsten", in *Gesammelte Studien zum Alten Testament*, 1957, pp. 274–90).

and turned aside, refusing to obey thy voice. And the curse and oath which are written in the law of Moses the servant of God have been poured out upon us, because we have sinned against him" (9.11). The prayer makes a simple and direct appeal to the mercy of God, and to his regard for his own name (vv. 9, 17, 19); but there are also hints that human agencies may engage in the work of expiation. Outstanding among the people, according to Daniel, are the משכילים, the teachers.[16] According to Daniel 11.35, these men shall stumble, or fall. The probable meaning is that they will die as martyrs, as the use of the same verb (נכשל) in v. 33 ("They shall fall by sword and flame, by captivity and plunder") shows. What is the effect of their martyrdom? According to the LXX, their suffering will result in their own cleansing (11.35):

... εἰς τὸ καθαρίσαι ἑαυτοὺς καὶ εἰς τὸ ἐκλεγῆναι καὶ εἰς τὸ καθαρισθῆναι ἕως καιροῦ συντελείας.

The R.S.V. text here on the whole follows the Greek in rendering:

... to refine and to cleanse them and to make them white until the time of the end.

As the R.S.V. margin notes, however, this is not the sense of the Hebrew, which after לצרף (= εἰς τὸ καθαρίσαι, to cleanse) reads not a direct object but בהם, among them, that is, among the people. Both interpretations find support in other passages. The Greek is supported by 12.10, where in both Greek and Hebrew the verbs are in the passive:

ἕως ἂν πειρασθῶσι καὶ ἁγιασθῶσι πολλοί = ויצרפו רבים (until many are tried and cleansed).

---

[16] This meaning of משכיל seems now to be established by the Dead Sea MSS. "So konnte das Wort *maskil* schliesslich in der Bedeutung 'Lehrer' verstanden werden ... Dies ist die biblische Vorgeschichte des Begriffes *maskil*, und es ist interessant, dass er schliesslich im Buche Daniel so gut wie fertig vorliegt. Von hier aus können wir dann auch die Aufgabe des *maskil* der Sekte erst richtig verstehen ... Die Übersetzung 'Verständiger', 'Weiser' ist also unzureichend ..." (H. Kosmala, *Hebräer—Essener—Christen*, Studia Post-Biblica I, 1959, p. 284).

This suggests that the wise themselves are purified by their own suffering. But 12.3 points in the other direction, for here the משכילים (teachers) are described in parallel as מצדיקי הרבים, "the justifiers of many" (they that turn many to righteousness).[17] "This verse refers to the teachers and leaders of the faithful. Amongst these would naturally be the martyrs and confessors of Judaism".[18] Here these leaders in their suffering purify, make righteous, not themselves but others—"many"; that is, the people as a whole, whom they will lead in the resurrection and glory (12.2) as they have led them in suffering.

There is nothing inconsistent in these two lines of thought, and it is probable that both were entertained by the author of Daniel. It is certain that elsewhere the sufferings of the Maccabean martyrs were taken to be propitiatory and expiatory,[19] and in rabbinic thought generally a man's sufferings, including death, were thought to make atonement for his own sins, with the possibility, in the case of the righteous, that a superfluity of merit (זכות) might accrue, and be used for the benefit of others. What is important for us to grasp is that Daniel, and the kind of thought it represents, is like a high mountain range in which rise several rivers, whose ultimate course will lead in very different directions. Here arises the apocalyptic figure of the Son of man, who in later apocalyptic will achieve far more by way of personal distinctness and individuation. Here the notion of apocalyptic suffering attains historical concreteness; that is, a particular period of suffering for certain definite historical persons is integrated into an eschatological world-view. Here is the conviction that the people of God will be vindicated, not in terms of historical development but by a divine act at the end of history, involving the resurrection of the dead, or at least of some of them. Here too is the notion, in embryonic form, of vicarious and atoning suffering. These themes are not developed, or wrought into a

---

[17] The Greek here, οἱ κατισχύοντες τοὺς λόγους μου, is far too remote from the Hebrew to be helpful.

[18] R. H. Charles, *The Book of Daniel*, Century Bible, n.d., p. 140.

[19] See *New Testament Essays* (above, n. 9), pp. 12f.

systematic whole; but they are present, and they arise in the same context.

That this observation is important for the study of the New Testament seems to me beyond question. It is not necessary to reinterpret "Son of man" in terms of "Servant of the Lord" in order to understand the predictions of the passion, and the passion itself. The themes of apocalyptic suffering (this, or eschatological suffering, may be a better term than "messianic affliction", since no personal messiah is necessarily involved, and the idea of a suffering messiah is notoriously difficult to establish in Judaism),[20] of a divine vindication,[21] manifestly supernatural in origin since its primary scene is with the clouds of heaven, of a Son of man figure, and of atonement, have common roots. This conclusion is undoubtedly important, though we must be careful not to exaggerate its importance. We have encountered the terminology, perhaps more than the terminology of the gospels, but it is present as raw, unformed and unworked, material. What the evangelists have to say in the language they inherited remains to be considered, but it is important to observe that means existed by which Jesus could interpret his own (or others') suffering "in the same eschatological context in which he interpreted his ministry as a whole" (p. 38).

The problem we are dealing with in this lecture is a very complicated one. It involves historical issues, for we are obliged to consider (however inadequate the data) the intention of Jesus in going up for the last time to Jerusalem, and the events which took place when he reached the city; and it involves also the successive interpretations of these events which are given in successive strata of the tradition. It is thus a special case of the problem set out in more general terms in the first lecture—the problem of the relation between historical and non-

---

20 See n. 8 above. "Messianic affliction" (not "affliction of the Messiah" —see J. Bonsirven, *Le Judaïsme palestinien*, 1934, i, p. 309 n. 1) is of course a natural rendering of חבלו של משיח.

21 For this theme see C. F. D. Moule in *Studiorum Novi Testamenti Societas: Bulletin III*, 1952, pp. 40–53.

historical elements in the tradition, and the significance of their juxtaposition. We may recall the Pauline formula of 1 Corinthians 15.3: "Christ died for our sins according to the Scriptures". The material in the gospels falls so far short of this in clarity of theological formulation, that we may not unreasonably expect to find something of historical worth embedded in it, and thus to find at least traces of what happened in the last hours of Jesus' life, and conceivably even of what these events meant to him.

We shall approach the problem by asking three questions.

1. Did Jesus think that he must die? To ask this question at this stage is to reopen an issue that might seem to have been settled at an earlier point, when it was shown that there was nothing improbable in the view that Jesus foresaw his suffering, and that if he foresaw it he must either have interpreted it in the context of his mission at large, and of the kingdom of God, or have withdrawn from public activity. If the issue is reopened this is because there are further facts in the gospels, and in particular in the passion narratives, that require this. We can look at only a few of these facts. The most important is the Gethsemane narrative (Mark 14.32–42). Here Jesus prays (v. 36): "Abba, Father, all things are possible to thee. Take this cup away from me. Yet not what I desire, but what thou [desirest]." The cup can be nothing other than the cup of suffering, presumably of death;[22] that is, Jesus prays that he may not have to suffer and die. It is true that his prayer is qualified by loyal and obedient acceptance of the Father's will, whatever it may be; yet it is offered. How is the prayer (if we may for the present accept its historicity, about which serious doubt has been expressed) to be understood? It may be taken as certain that Jesus' hope was not that a convenient way of escape might open up, so that he might slip away unobserved and so avoid the final peril. Not only is this in contradiction with the sense of the narrative; if Jesus had wished to escape he

---

[22] Not necessarily of wrath; see M. Black, "The Cup Metaphor in Mark xiv.36", in *Expository Times*, lix, p. 195.

could in all probability have done so. He does not appear even to have tried. His prayer must imply that he was at least contemplating the possibility that the wished-for future, the establishing of the kingdom of God, might come without the necessity of preliminary suffering.

Did Jesus then up to the last moment hope that God would intervene and deliver him by inaugurating the age to come? There is ground for thinking that he did in the extraordinary fact, stated by Mark and taken over by Matthew and Luke, that notwithstanding Jesus' repeated injunctions to stay awake, all his disciples, even the three whom he took to be with him during his prayer, fell asleep. This is scarcely credible. However little the disciples understood of the real intentions of Jesus, they did understand that they were in a crucial situation involving real danger. At least one or two of them were armed (Mark 14.47; cf. Luke 22.36,38). In these circumstances men may run away, but they do not normally fall asleep. It may well be that this feature of the narrative is due to misunderstanding of the command, γρηγορεῖτε (Mark 14.34,38). Ordinarily this word means "Keep awake", and would be addressed to men who were dropping off to sleep, and might, notwithstanding the injunction, lose consciousness. But in the New Testament (Matt. 24.42; 25.13; Mark 13.35,37; 1 Cor. 16.13; 1 Thess. 5.10; 1 Pet. 5.8; Rev. 3.2,3; 16.15; cf. Matt. 24.43; Mark 13.34; Luke 12.37) it may bear the specific meaning of watching for the *parousia* of Christ, or, more generally, for eschatological events, and it may be that the strange story in the gospels is due to misunderstanding. The evangelists mistakenly turned into a command to remain physically awake an exhortation to look out for the long-expected fulfilment of the apocalyptic hope, and went on to draw the inference that those to whom the command was addressed were falling asleep.

It is hard to think that we have a precise account of the words spoken by Jesus in Gethsemane (for who heard them?), but it is equally unlikely that this urgent—and disappointed—apocalyptic hope was gratuitously invented by the evangelists. This interpretation is supported by two facts, one based on the

Jewish background of the events in question, and one arising directly out of the gospels.

In the first place, there is some evidence for a Jewish belief that the Messiah would come, and the messianic deliverance take place, in Passover night. The evidence for this has been collected by Dr Jeremias;[23] it rests ultimately upon Exodus 12.42: ליל שמרים הוא ליהוה, which originally meant, "a night to be observed in the Lord's honour", but was understood to mean, "a night in which one watches for the Lord". In Mekhilta on this passage R. Joshua ben Hananya (c. A.D. 90) says: "In this night they were redeemed, and in this night they shall be redeemed". According to the synoptic gospels, it was the Passover supper Jesus and his disciples left to go to Gethsemane; there is therefore nothing surprising in the view that at least some of them were in a state of intense eschatological excitement and expectation.

In the second place, according to Mark Jesus died with words on his lips that are most naturally understood as expressing disappointment: "My God, my God, why hast thou forsaken me?" (Mark 15.34). A full study of these words would take far more time than we can spare, but they make sense if Jesus had been expecting God to act in his vindication before his death, and knew now that his hope was to be disappointed.

There is thus some reason to think that, though in the course of the tradition other themes masked the original motifs of the narrative, Jesus, as late as his last night on earth, hoped, perhaps believed, that God would intervene to vindicate him and establish his kingdom before the extremity of death. If, however, this conclusion is valid, what of the argument conducted above to show that both prediction and interpretation of impending suffering are conceivable? In particular, what of the immediately preceding narrative of the Supper, in which Jesus appears to be calmly contemplating his death? Did he suddenly lose his nerve as the reality of arrest, torture, and death was borne in upon him? It might suffice to say that if this was so

---

[23] J. Jeremias, *The Eucharistic Words of Jesus*, 1966, pp. 205ff.; also *Theologisches Wörterbuch zum Neuen Testament*, Vol. V, p. 901.

Jesus was a less worthy man than many who have suffered as martyrs in his cause; but we can say more. Whatever the Gethsemane story, at any stage in its traditional development, may suggest, it does not suggest failure of nerve, but rather firm determination, even in the face of disappointment.

So much for our first question. At this stage it is my intention to leave it as a question, with the observation that, if we use it as a tool for the historical investigation of the passion material, what it discloses proves to be anything but a unitary and consistent whole. In the first twelve chapters of Mark we encounter the frequently repeated prediction that Jesus must suffer and die; in the passion narrative (chapters 14 and 15) suffering and death take at least the disciples by surprise.

2. If for the moment we confine our attention to that part of the traditional material (and it is by far the greater part) that suggests that Jesus did expect to suffer and die, a further question suggests itself: did he expect to die alone, or in the company of his disciples, or some of them? The first major prediction of the passion (Mark 8.31) is followed almost immediately by sayings about discipleship:

> If anyone wishes to come after me, let him deny himself and take up his cross: that is how he must follow me. For whoever wishes to save himself, shall lose himself; and whoever loses himself for my sake and the Gospel's, shall save himself. For what good does it do a man to gain the whole world and lose himself? For what compensation is a man to give in exchange for himself? (Mark 8.34–7).

These words are not completely clear, and have probably been affected already by the process which has made the Lucan form (with its reference to taking up one's cross *daily*[24]) more "edifying" than the Marcan. But if they have any historical value at all and can be read in the context of the ministry, they can hardly mean less than that discipleship is likely to end in

[24] Luke's form of the saying certainly implies the regular discipline of the Christian life rather than a challenge to share a specific fate in a particular historical situation.

crucifixion.[25] Apparently, when they were spoken, Jesus did not expect to die alone.

In Mark 10.35–40 there is even more explicit material. James and John ask to be allowed to sit on the right and left of Jesus in his glory. Such favours Jesus cannot grant; the seats have already been allocated. Instead he asks the two disciples if they can drink his cup, and be baptized with the baptism with which he himself is to be baptized. Not only do they profess their ability to do this, Jesus affirms that they shall. That the cup (cf. Mark 14.36) and baptism (cf. Luke 12.50) refer to suffering is hardly open to doubt, and there is in the narrative itself no hint that James and John are to suffer many years after Jesus; rather it seems to be expected that they will drink from the same cup and pass through the same waters at the same time.

To these explicit words may be added features of the passion narrative, especially the Last Supper. The significance of commensality in ancient, and perhaps especially in Semitic, society is well known.

> Every stranger whom one meets in the desert is a natural enemy, and has no protection against violence except his own strong hand or the fear that his tribe will avenge him if his blood be spilt. But if I have eaten the smallest morsel of food with a man, I have nothing further to fear from him; "there is salt between us", and he is bound not only to do me no harm, but to help and defend me as if I were his brother . . . The temporary bond is confirmed by repetition, and readily passes into a permanent tie confirmed by an oath.[26]

The disciples ate with Jesus, and the relation formed by common eating was made yet more close and firm in that it included a sharing of blood;[27] and part of the significance of the common meal is that those who ate with Jesus should have been prepared if not to defend him at least to die with him. Thus Jesus takes his disciples with him into Gethsemane, and expects them

---

[25] Unless at this time Jesus expected not only to die, but to die at the hands of the Romans, his prediction must have undergone some rewriting.

[26] W. R. Smith, *The Religion of the Semites*, 1901, pp. 269f. Cf. J. G. Frazer, *The Golden Bough*, abridged edn, 1963, p. 266.

[27] See Frazer, loc. cit.; and Smith, op. cit. pp. 312–20, 479–81.

to keep watch (Mark 14.32f., 37). There is some evidence of a readiness to offer some kind of defence (Mark 14.47), but long before the moment of crucifixion the disciples have taken to their heels, in treacherous denial of the covenant into which they had entered.

This is one strain that runs through the gospels: however gross their eventual failure, the disciples had been expected to follow their master to the bitter end. But this is not the only strain. Only half a dozen verses after the prediction that James and John should drink his cup and be baptized with his baptism, in Mark 10.45 Jesus declares that the Son of man (and for Mark this undoubtedly means Jesus) will give his life as a λύτρον ἀντὶ πολλῶν (ransom for many); that is, he will suffer and die in place of others in order that they may escape, that they may not die. In the Last Supper (which we have just regarded from another angle) he speaks of his blood as poured out ὑπὲρ πολλῶν (on behalf of many), and here (notwithstanding the different preposition) the meaning is substantially the same. And, in fact, none of his disciples died with Jesus.

In the gospels as they stand, as documents belonging to the latter part of the first century, there is an explanation of this apparent contradiction ready to hand. The disciples did not die, and were not expected to die, with, that is, at the same time as, Jesus, but later they endured suffering on his behalf as martyrs. The time scheme is made clear in the apocalypse of Mark 13. This apocalypse, surprisingly (if one is to think of it as a set of predictions made by Jesus on the eve of his passion) makes no reference to his own approaching death. It is clear, however, that it presupposes his departure from the start, for already in 13.5f. there is a warning against deception by those who come "in my name". If they come "in the name" of Jesus, they come in his absence.[28] After Jesus' departure in

---

[28] The argument that in Mark 13.6 ἐγώ εἰμι means not "It is I" but "It is Jesus!" (W. Manson, "The ΕΓΩ ΕΙΜΙ of the Messianic Presence in the New Testament", in *Journal of Theological Studies*, Vol. xlviii, pp. 137–45; D. Daube, *The New Testament and Rabbinic Judaism*, 1956, pp. 325–9) is not convincing. ἐπὶ τῷ ὀνόματί μου means, "pretending to be myself".

death, therefore, the disciples must expect, in addition to sufferings which they will share with the human race as a whole, to be punished by Jewish authorities (synagogue courts) and Gentile authorities (governors and kings). They will incur universal hatred, and that even in their own families. This chapter (whatever its sources may have been) undoubtedly sets forth Mark's own understanding of the matter. Jesus first suffers on behalf of others, and departs in death; later his disciples will suffer persecution in their service to him—a neat rationalization but one that scarcely does justice to the traditional material Mark himself preserves, though within the new framework forced upon him by the actual course of events.

The same comment may be made on another attempt to simplify and explain the diverse data of the gospels. Dr Schweitzer's view[29] is that when Jesus sent out his disciples on their preaching and healing mission he believed that their work would precipitate the period of apocalyptic suffering and the end itself. Hence, in the mission charge of Matthew 10 there occur predictions of suffering for disciples, and the prophecy (10.23) that they should not have completed their work in all the cities of Israel before the coming of the Son of man. Jesus did not expect to see them back in the present age; yet they returned, with no sign of the apocalyptic climax. He was obliged to rethink his position, and came to the conclusion that his disciples were unable to join him in the task of evoking and enduring the apocalyptic woes; he must therefore take the whole burden on his own shoulders, suffering himself that the rest might go free. Thus the predictions of corporate suffering, and of individual suffering, belong to different periods in the teaching of Jesus. This is an impressive suggestion, and one that contains a considerable measure of truth, but it too is an oversimplification of the data. As has often been pointed out, it rests too heavily upon Matthew 10, which is evidently as composite and artificial a discourse as that of Mark 13;[30] and it does not take account of the fact that the two themes, whose

---

[29] See especially *The Mystery of the Kingdom of God*, 1925, pp. 230–6.

[30] In fact, they share, to some extent, the same material.

apparent inconsistency creates our problem, both run on into the passion narrative itself.

Our second question thus leads to a position similar to that to which we were brought by the first; and for the present we must be content with confusion, and tension, between two opposite answers.

3. On what charge, by whose instigation, and under whose authority, did Jesus die? This is a complicated question, but it is more objective than those we have now discussed, for it deals with straightforward questions of fact, not with hopes, fears, expectations, and thoughts of Jesus, concerning which we can at the best entertain provisional and conjectural hypotheses. It has been given fresh sharpness and prominence by Paul Winter's book, *On the Trial of Jesus*,[31] which still awaits a serious reply.[32]

Detailed investigation is out of the question here; only a few significant points can be brought out. First, it stands out unmistakably that, when we read the passion narratives in what we may take to be the order of composition—first Mark, then Matthew and Luke, and finally John—there appears to be a progressive attempt to lighten the responsibility of the Romans for the crucifixion of Jesus, and to increase that of the Jews. Already in Mark Pilate is not a willing participant in the condemnation of Jesus. He asks, surprised, what evil Jesus has done (15.14), and tries to secure his release under a custom for whose existence we have no independent evidence (15.6–10); but his aim is to please the people, and when their will is clear he acts with little hesitation (15.15). Matthew introduces into the Marcan story (a source he follows closely) the references to Pilate's wife and her dream (27.19) and to Pilate's symbolic washing of his hands (27.24). According to Luke, Pilate

31 P. Winter, *On the Trial of Jesus*, 1961.
32 A. N. Sherwin-White, *Roman Society and Roman Law in the New Testament*, 1963, p. 47, claims to have refuted Winter in advance. This is an optimistic estimate. Among earlier, but very important works, see especially G. D. Kilpatrick, *The Trial of Jesus*, 1953, and J. Blinzler, *The Trial of Jesus*, 1959.

5

repeatedly protested the innocence of Jesus, and twice proposed
the minor punishment of beating and release[33] (23.16,22). He
failed to throw off his responsibility upon Herod, but succeeded
at least in winning Herod's agreement that Jesus was innocent
(23.15). In the end he merely permitted the Jews to have *their*
way (παρέδωκεν τῷ θελήματι αὐτῶν, handed him over to their
will, 23.25). John is theologically more cautious and historically
more forceful. He cannot represent Pilate as being actually
"of the truth" (18.37f.), but he emphasizes his uprightness and
sympathy. He pronounces Jesus innocent (18.38; 19.6), and it
is only when the Jews employ the unanswerable argument,
"If you release this man you are not Caesar's friend", that
Pilate gives up his attempt to release Jesus (19.12).

Correspondingly, the Jews are blackened. In Matthew they
cry out, "His blood be upon us, and upon our children"
(27.25). In Luke we must distinguish between the mass of the
people, who show sympathy with Jesus (23.27), and their rulers,
who bring a more detailed charge than appears in any other
gospel, a charge which Luke certainly thinks of as a deliberate
lie—Jesus had prevented the payment of tribute to Caesar
(23.2). In John, Jesus himself says to Pilate, "He that handed
me over to you [the high priest, if we are to name a single
person] has the greater guilt" (19.11). Nothing could be more
explicit.

As we pass from Mark to John there appears a clear tendency
to exonerate or excuse Pilate, and to fasten the guilt of the
death of Jesus more firmly upon the Jews. There is no reason to
suppose that this tendency began after, or with, the writing of
Mark, and we may therefore suppose that in pre-Marcan
tradition the Jews appeared less and the Romans more responsible for the crucifixion, and that this probably corresponded
to the facts. We must, however, draw this conclusion with caution,
remembering that in one of the earliest New Testament
documents, written long before the earliest gospel, Paul declares that the Jews killed the Lord Jesus (1 Thess. 2.15).

[33] Sherwin-White, op. cit. pp. 27f.

Whatever the legal position, the Jews rejected Jesus—a fact that must be borne in mind in any historical reconstruction.

Secondly, the issue brought before Pilate's court can be stated much more clearly than the discussions supposed to have taken place before the Sanhedrin. According to Luke, in a passage already referred to (23.2), Jesus is alleged to have been inciting disaffection among the Jewish people, preventing the payment of tribute, and giving himself out to be the Messiah—in plain western language, a king. This may be derived from an independent Lucan source, but is better explained as an expansion of Mark 15.2, where it is implied that Pilate has been told that Jesus claimed to be a king. The same theme is found in John, and indeed, when the characteristically Johannine discussion of truth is removed, it stands out there with exceptional clarity, and is reflected in the dramatic words (19.14), ἴδε ὁ βασιλεὺς ὑμῶν (Here is your king). All this is clear, and makes good sense. Roman governors were not theological inquisitors but, if they were worthy of their office, they had a quick ear for such *minutio maiestatis* and such peril to Roman peace, as were involved in a claim to kingship. On no other charge (except the closely related charges of public disturbance and *contumacia*) would a Roman be likely to act; on this one he could not fail to do so. Since Jesus was crucified, and therefore executed by Romans, it is highly probable that we have here the charge preferred in the Roman court, and that there did appear on or near the cross some such form of words as "Jesus of Nazareth, the king of the Jews". There are obscure and dubious details in the narrative of Jesus before Pilate, but so much at least is clear and secure. Whatever may have happened earlier in the ministry, in the passion narrative the theme of messiahship comes to the front. This supports the view (cf. pp. 22ff., 28, 30, 34) that, though Jesus did not claim messiahship, others (enemies as well as friends) were able to see messianic significance in his actions.

What happened before Jesus was brought to the procurator? The course of events is far from clear, and the obscurity of the outline does nothing to add credit to the details. According to

Mark (closely followed by Matthew) Jesus was, immediately after his arrest, brought before the high priest, who was accompanied by all the chief priests, elders, and scribes, that is, by the whole Sanhedrin[34] (not a sub-committee of the main body). Luke has no such night meeting, and occupies the night solely with the narrative of Peter's denial, which Mark interweaves with the "first trial". John has a narrative which possesses notorious obscurities of its own but is not at this stage radically distinguished from Mark's. Early morning is reached at Matthew 27.1; Mark 15.1; Luke 22.66. At this point Luke places his first (and only) Jewish trial. Matthew says that the Jewish authorities "took counsel" ($\sigma\upsilon\mu\beta\upsilon\acute{\lambda}\iota\upsilon\nu$ $\check{\epsilon}\lambda\alpha\beta\upsilon\nu$)—presumably held another meeting; this is no doubt Matthew's reading of Mark, where there is textual uncertainty,[35] though even if Mark means that they "prepared a plan" presumably they did so at a meeting of some kind. According to John 18.28 Jesus was taken early in the morning from Caiaphas to Pilate's Praetorium.

Our sources are thus divided, and it would in my opinion be rash to suppose that there were two full, formal meetings of the judicial Sanhedrin, one in the course of the night, and another in the early morning. It would equally, I think, be unwise to follow Luke (who probably is merely simplifying Mark) in thinking that there was only one meeting and that it took place in the morning. It is unlikely that many leading members of the Sanhedrin got much sleep that night. We can say little more than that between the close of the Passover meal and his appearance before Pilate next morning, Jesus appeared before the high priest and at least some of his colleagues, and that a case was prepared for submission to the Procurator.[36] This is

---

[34] Mark 14.53: $\pi\acute{\alpha}\nu\tau\epsilon\varsigma$ $o\acute{\iota}$ $\dot{\alpha}\rho\chi\iota\epsilon\rho\epsilon\hat{\iota}\varsigma$, $\kappa\tau\lambda$.

[35] Mark 15.1: $\sigma\upsilon\mu\beta\upsilon\acute{\lambda}\iota\upsilon\nu$ $\dot{\epsilon}\tau\upsilon\iota\mu\acute{\alpha}\sigma\alpha\nu\tau\epsilon\varsigma$ (they prepared a plan), $\aleph$ C pc; the rest have either $\sigma\upsilon\mu\beta\upsilon\acute{\lambda}\iota\upsilon\nu$ $\pi\upsilon\iota\acute{\eta}\sigma\alpha\nu\tau\epsilon\varsigma$ or $\sigma\upsilon\mu\beta\upsilon\acute{\lambda}\iota\upsilon\nu$ $\dot{\epsilon}\pi\upsilon\acute{\iota}\eta\sigma\alpha\nu$ ... $\kappa\alpha\acute{\iota}$ (they held a council meeting).

[36] There is much to be said for the view that all the gospel narratives "telescope" the events of the trial and execution, but this, if established, would strengthen rather than weaken the conclusions drawn here. See M. Black, "The Arrest and Trial of Jesus and the Date of the Last Supper", in *New Testament Essays* (see n. 10 above), pp. 19–33.

implied by the fact that leading Jews appear as *delatores* in Pilate's court. The charge they laid before Pilate was, as we have seen, that Jesus claimed to be the anointed king of the Jews, and as such was advocating rebellion against Rome. Was this an honest representation of the conviction of the Jewish authorities, or was it a deliberate misrepresentation both of Jesus and of the Jewish complaint against him, framed with a view to securing a conviction? It is difficult to answer this question, because the narrative is clouded by two factors: anti-Jewish prejudice on the part of the evangelists and their predecessors in handing on the tradition, and their conviction (which was at least an over-simplification) that Jesus had truly been the Messiah, even though a secret Messiah.

In Mark the following features of the narrative can be discerned.

(*a*) The failure of the Sanhedrin to find satisfactory evidence against Jesus (14.55–9). Even false witnesses could produce no agreed story. It is natural to see in this comment a piece of Christian apologetic: the innocence of Jesus was so secure that not even false testimony could shake it. But this conclusion may be too simple. Mark implies that the Sanhedrin was too concerned for truth and justice to allow itself to be swayed by evidence that was not consistent with itself, and this does not look like a Christian invention. We should perhaps infer that the Sanhedrin never published evidence submitted at its examination of Jesus. The evangelists therefore did not know what the evidence was, but were sure that it must have been false.

(*b*) The only direct evidence brought against Jesus in Mark is the allegation that he had said, "I will destroy this man-made temple, and in three days I will build another that is not man-made" (14.58; cf. 15.29). Matthew, unlike Mark, does not describe this as false testimony, and changes the future "I will destroy" into the less disturbing "I can destroy". In view of John 2.19 it seems probable that Jesus did predict the destruction and renewal of the temple, and this prediction may have figured in his trial, though its presence in the Marcan story may well be due to inference rather than accurate knowledge on Mark's part.

(c) After the failure (according to Mark) to secure convincing evidence, the high priest interrogates his prisoner, at first indirectly, and unsuccessfully (14.60f.), then in a direct question. In Matthew and Mark it is a double question; in Luke there are two separate questions. Jesus is asked whether he is the Messiah, the Son of God. These two terms would mean different things to the high priest and to the evangelists. To the former, the Messiah would suggest a political figure, bearing the title Son of God as a mark of his human dignity. The latter understood Messiah in a religious sense, and gave Son of God a metaphysical content. The situation is further complicated by the fact that, though Jesus gives an affirmative answer, he goes on to expand it in terms of a third title, Son of man. It is in harmony with Mark's total presentation of the messiahship of Jesus that Jesus should affirm it positively only at the moment when none of his hearers could possibly believe him, and even then abandon the theme of messiahship for the preferred title Son of man; but whether even so much can be judged historical is open to question.

(d) After Jesus' avowal of messiahship the high priest claims that he has spoken blasphemy in the hearing of the Council. This, if we may follow the regulations of the Mishnah, he had not done.[37] So far from pronouncing the sacred tetragrammaton he had carefully avoided (according to Mark) using even the word God, and had spoken of the Son of man as sitting on the right hand of "the Power" (14.62). It may be that the word blasphemy is used in a loose sense (as perhaps at Mark' 2.7); but blasphemy in this loose sense, however objectionable to Jewish sentiment, could hardly be taken as adequate ground for a death sentence.

This relatively muddled state of the account of the trial before the Jewish authorities strongly suggests a lack of first-hand

---

[37] Sanhedrin 7.5: "The blasphemer" (Lev. 24.10ff.) is not culpable unless he pronounces the Name itself.

knowledge, and a not too well informed reconstruction of what Christians, in Mark's time and later, supposed must have happened. The comparatively clear account of the charge before the procuratorial court goes far to support Dr Winter's contenion that the real legal business was between Jesus and Pilate.[38]

A third observation about the passion story is that the death of Jesus appears to have broken the spirit and the loyalty of the disciples. Up to a late point in the narrative as we have it they profess that not even death will cause them to deny or desert Jesus; Peter is specially loud in his protestations, but he is joined by the whole group (Mark 14.31). Yet in the end, all the disciples desert Jesus, Peter denies him, and Judas betrays him. This regrettable behaviour may have been due to simple fear of death or other punishment. It seems probable, however, that so complete a debacle had deeper roots, and it is at least consistent with some element of surprise in the situation. Men keyed up to face one kind of danger may suddenly collapse if threatened from an unexpected quarter. The reaction of the disciples seems to demand that they had not understood Jesus to predict that he would die, and that his death would be followed after a very short period by his reanimation, and to suggest that the manner of his arrest and the substance of the charge brought against him were not what they had expected.

Finally, we may note the setting of Jesus' execution. He was crucified between two λῃσταί, robbers (Mark 15.27); but the λῃσταί were in all probability not mere bandits but armed rebels, attempting to overthrow the government.[39] The

---

38 "It can be affirmed with assurance that Jesus was arrested by Roman military personnel (John 18.12) for political reasons (Mark 14.48; John 18.20) ... The following morning, after a brief deliberation by the Jewish authorities, he was handed back to the Romans for trial (Mark 15.1; Luke 22.66; 23.1; John 18.28a). The procurator sentenced Jesus to death by crucifixion (Tacitus; Mark 15.15b, 26), the sentence being carried out in accordance with Roman penal procedure (Mark 15.15b, 24a, 27)" (op. cit. pp. 137f.).

39 See K. H. Rengstorf in *Theologisches Wörterbuch zum Neuen Testament*, Vol. IV, pp. 262–7, especially p. 263: "Bei Josephus ist λῃστής die ständige Bezeichnung der *Zeloten*, die den bewaffneten Kampf gegen die römische Herrschaft ... zum Inhalt ihres Lebens gemacht haben."

prisoner whose release the crowd demanded instead of Jesus' was Barabbas, one who was in prison along with the revolutionaries (στασιασταί), the men who had committed murder in the revolution (ἐν τῇ στάσει, Mark 15.7). It is reasonable to note the definite article, and to ask, "In which revolution?" And it is not unreasonable to guess that the answer is, "A revolution or revolt that had been taking place at the same Passover as that at which Jesus was arrested". This does not justify us in embarking with Eisler[40] on an imaginative reconstruction of events, including the mining of the Tower in Siloam, and so forth. But it does suggest that, at the time of the crucifixion, there existed a very confused and confusing political situation, and that in this situation the intentions of Jesus may have been grievously misrepresented and seriously misunderstood. This may help to explain the sudden burst of royal and messianic language in the passion narratives, which, in this respect, contrast so sharply with other parts of the gospels; nevertheless, our third question does not lead to a more clearcut answer than the first and second.

Study of these, and of related problems, may lead to the conclusion that the gospels as they stand are in a state of hopeless confusion. When the way seems to have been cleared for acceptance of Jesus' predictions of his suffering and death as historical and authentic, at least in outline, we observe that the disciples cannot have understood him to make such predictions, especially if (as the gospels say) he accompanied them by prophecies of his resurrection on the third day, since these events found them completely unprepared. Moreover, it seems from a number of hints preserved in the passion narrative that Jesus himself was not fully convinced that his death must precede the glorious consummation. We read on the one hand that Jesus intended to give his life as a ransom for others, to die that they might live, and on the other that he expected his disciples to share his fate and perish with him. The gospels agree that Jesus died a Roman death, and therefore at the hand of the Roman

[40] R. Eisler, *The Messiah Jesus and John the Baptist*, 1931—a book whose learning is not neutralized by its lapses from sound judgement.

authorities, but they also represent Jesus as found liable to the death penalty by the supreme Jewish court, not on the count of pretended messiahship but, presumably, on that of blasphemy, though the trial narratives give no hint of blasphemy in the technical sense. The gospel story as a whole records many controversies of Jesus with Jews, and none with Romans, but in the passion narrative it is the case of the Romans against Jesus that can be clearly stated.

How is this disorderly state of our sources to be explained? In the first place, as far as the "trials" are concerned, both Jewish and Roman, genuine historical information drawn from first-hand authorities must have been very scarce. The hypothesis that members of the Sanhedrin, converted after the crucifixion and resurrection,[41] may have supplied their Christian brethren with the desired information cannot be disproved, but it loses probability when the different forms of the tradition in Mark, Luke, and John are considered. It is probable that the evangelists were to a great extent reduced to the expedient of drawing inferences from the judicial procedures of the respective courts, and these were probably very imperfectly known to them—this certainly seems a reasonable conclusion from the texts. Conjecture on the basis of sheer ignorance of the facts goes far to accounting for the narratives in the gospels.

It goes far, but it does not go all the way. The superficially inharmonious appearance of the passion material in the gospels is due to some extent to the underlying facts themselves; for the imperfection of the narratives must not lead us to forget that underlying facts there undoubtedly were. It is as certain that Jesus was crucified as that Caesar crossed the Rubicon; judicial processes of some kind were involved, and Jesus himself, his disciples, and his adversaries must have formulated some view of the meaning of events, in prospect, and as they took place. Even if the course of events can no longer be precisely traced, the events stand behind our narratives, and there

41 Cf. Acts 6.7.

is no good reason to suppose that they formed a simple and self-explanatory sequence, or that all the participants understood them in the same way.

This leads to the second main point. In Lecture 1, I tried to establish that the confused state of the gospel tradition in general is due to the fact that it reflects more than one historical period. This is true of the tradition about the passion in particular, and we now have the opportunity of illustrating the point in some detail. We may begin from the observation that Jesus was involved in conflict with both Jews and Romans, and this twofold conflict led up to and reached its climax in the cross, and the parallel observation that the early Church also was involved in conflict with both Jews and Romans, and its twofold conflict followed upon and arose out of the cross.

The conflict between Jesus and Judaism arose out of the authority with which Jesus acted and taught—authority which he refused to explain or ground in any official position, but authority which equally he refused to renounce. Both the positive and negative aspects of this fact we have already studied in Lecture 1.[42] It comes most clearly to light in the disputes between Jesus and the Jewish authorities over the Law. This is a difficult and delicate question, and one that can only be hinted at here. Dr Winter seems to me to be correct in saying that, in most matters arising out of the Law, Jesus taught and acted as a Pharisee;[43] but the matter cannot be left there, for our sources too often represent Jesus as engaged in controversy with the Pharisees for us to dismiss these conflicts as merely imaginary constructions, based on conflicts which took place later in the time of the Church. Moreover, the subjects of dispute are different; the Sabbath does not appear to have been a major subject of dispute between Paul and his Judaizing opponents, but it bulks largely in the conflict stories in the gospels. The theme is important, because it illustrates the way in which Jesus is to be distinguished from Pharisaism.

[42] See pp. 28ff.

[43] Winter, op. cit. p. 120: "Jesus himself in his teaching stood closer to early Pharisaism than to any other school of thought." (Cf. pp. 132f.)

We may take as an example the story of the man with a withered hand (Mark 3.1–6). After the scene has been set, Jesus asks, "Is it lawful on the Sabbath to do good, or to do evil? to save life, or to kill?" Mark adds, "They were silent". It is not surprising. On the common presuppositions of rabbinic Judaism the questions were virtually unanswerable because they scarcely made sense. The relevant Jewish presuppositions, and the immediate inferences, were these. (*a*) It is always right (by definition) to do good. (*b*) It is never right (by definition) to do evil. (*c*) Saving life is a good, which should be done; and killing is an evil, which should not be done. (*d*) Observance of the Sabbath also is a good, which should be done. (*e*) So far as possible, a man should do both these good things, by healing the sick from Sunday to Friday, and then observing the day of rest. (*f*) If life is in danger, then, in order to avoid the evil of taking life by neglecting to save it, but only is such emergencies, one should heal on the Sabbath also. This is as rational as it is religious, and a modern Christian doctor might well (*mutatis mutandis*) make the principle his own.

Now it is a significant feature of this narrative that the sick man is suffering from a withered hand—not a fatal disease. The one recognized justification for healing on the Sabbath is wanting. Jesus' question only makes sense if we can assume that what he was doing was "saving life" in a sense different from that of ordinary medical work. The argument thus moves on to different ground from that of conventional dispute about what is and what is not permitted on the Sabbath. Jesus, good Pharisee though in many respects he was, did not represent himself and his disciples as a third group, Jeshua and Beth Jeshua, who could be classed with Hillel and Beth Hillel, Shammai and Beth Shammai.

The fact is that here, and in the preaching of Jesus generally, there is an egoism that is inconsistent with good Jewish piety.[44]

[44] J. Klausner, *Jesus of Nazareth*, 1925, pp. 408f.: "Jesus possesses a belief in his mission which verges on the extreme of self-veneration ... So strong was Jesus' belief in himself that he came to rely upon himself more than upon any of Israel's great ones, even Moses."

This is pointedly expressed in, for example, the sayings in the Sermon on the Mount (Matt. 5.21ff.) where Jesus opposes himself and his own authority to the law of Moses. It may well be that editorial activity has sharpened the contrast here; the substance of it is already present in Mark 10.21, where Jesus says to a man who has professed obedience to the whole law, "You are still short of one thing. . . . Come, follow *me*". The law does not provide adequate direction for the people of God; its place must be taken by Jesus—and the fact that on ordinary occasions Jesus is willing enough to observe the law does not lessen the offence.

It is not only in the directing of obedience that Jesus replaces the law. He takes the place of the law as the means by which man is related to God. Thus in Mark 2.5, confronted by a paralytic let down through the roof, Jesus declares, "Your sins are forgiven", and the scribes observing are not slow to detect the blasphemy—and, on their own premises, they are right. In a case where the law has failed (since the man has sinned) Jesus claims to create the man's relation with God. Well-known critical objections[45] can be brought against the unity of Mark 2.1–12, and it may be that verses 5–10 are a secondary supplement. But the whole theme of the attitude of Jesus to outcasts, to publicans and sinners, cannot be removed from the gospels, and this theme bears witness to the claim of Jesus to supplant the Torah as the means by which the prodigal children find their way home to God. His ministry thus becomes a standing challenge to Israel, organized as a community in this world with God as an absentee landlord, organized with a view to obedience to the written and oral Torah. We fail to understand the situation in the gospels if we do not observe the difficult position in which this places both Jesus and the Jewish authorities. Jesus can only act as Lord, without being able formally to establish his claim. The Jews are confronted with a blasphemy that does not fall within the code of blasphemy. What is each to do?

---

[45] See V. Taylor, *The Gospel according to St Mark*, 1952, pp. 191f.

A temporary relief of this tension was found when Jesus was brought before the procurator's court on a charge of sedition. By what process Jesus was delated to the procurator it is difficult, perhaps impossible, now to say.[46] We have already seen that the gospel tradition increasingly laid the blame upon the Jews, but it would be quite unrealistic to deny that, if the Sanhedrin did not actually engineer the arrest of Jesus by the Romans, many of its members must have breathed a sigh of relief when the arrest took place. Probably the Sanhedrin was not as unanimous as Mark 14.64 suggests: Joseph of Arimathaea (Mark 15.43) seems at least to have been sympathetic, and Matthew (27.57) and Luke (23.50f.) were both sensitive to the difficulty involved in Mark's description of him as a councillor. No doubt it helped that there was a revolt at the time—the revolt in which Barabbas and his colleagues had committed murder. Jesus and his followers (some of whom were armed) cannot have been easily distinguishable from other groups. Hence the appearance of Jesus with the mocking title, "The King of the Jews", a title that contained a double mockery since it was one he had been careful not to claim. Probably it required only silence, the failure of any influential and accredited Jew to defend him, to secure his condemnation. And how could the Jews have defended one whose life and teaching cut at the roots of their religion? And how could the disciples be expected to stand by a cause they had never espoused, in circumstances they had never been led to contemplate?

Their turn was to come, and we must now look at their conflict with Jews and Romans.

The Church's conflict with the Jews was Christological. So had Jesus' own conflict been, but it was now formalized, and crystallized upon particular titles. These described offices which

---

46 P. Winter, op. cit. p. 147: "That the general responsibility for the execution of Jesus, like that for the execution of other persons condemned with or without trial for political crimes during Pilate's term of office, belonged to the procurator, is undeniable—and yet it is not unlikely that in Jesus' case members of the hierarchy had a hand in the affair as well."

Christians believed that Jesus occupied: he was the Messiah, and he was the Son of God. Jews denied both propositions. Thus the trial of Jesus before the Sanhedrin is made to turn upon these points. Jews believed Jesus to be guilty of blasphemy; Christians believed him to be Messiah and Son of God. Hence, according to Mark 14.64 (but in defiance of historical probability) Jesus is condemned for blasphemy on the grounds of the claim, put into his mouth, that he is Messiah and Son of God. As far as the Romans were concerned, it soon became the Church's aim to show that it was politically innocent. The theme of messiahship was a delicate and dangerous one. Convinced that Jesus was the fulfilment of the word of God in the Old Testament, the Church, not unnaturally, jumped to the conclusion that he was the fulfilment of the more elaborate hopes of post-biblical Judaism, and thus came to the conclusion that he must have been the expected Messiah. Nor was it wrong in doing so, for, as we have seen, if there are in the gospels no genuine messianic avowals, there are messianic hints. Moreover, from the Roman point of view Jesus had died as the Messiah, the King of the Jews. Several ways of dealing with this difficult problem may be distinguished, though I cannot develop them here. The most complicated, and in some ways, the nearest to history, is the complicated Marcan solution of the concealed messiahship; the easiest was the method of simply allowing the title to become a second proper name—Jesus Christ; the latest (so far as the New Testament goes) was the acceptance of the fact of Jesus' kingship with the insistence that it was an otherworldly kingship: "My kingdom is not of this world" (John 18.36).

By such courses as these the story of the death of Jesus, with the attendant predictions and interpretations, took shape. There are two points to add:

1. Dr Winter is right: the legal issue lay between Jesus and Pilate, not between Jesus and the Jews. The Church, moved in its transmission of the tradition by apologetic motives, tended to exonerate Pilate and to inculpate the Jews. This was a falsifica-

tion of historical data. Yet at the same time (and here I am illustrating the conclusion of Lecture 1) this process was based upon truth, and historical truth at that. It is true that the legal issue, the ground on which Pilate ordered the crucifixion, lay between Jesus and Pilate; true also that Jesus was innocent, for he was not and never intended to be the kind of king Pilate could legitimately punish. But the far more important theological issue lay between Jesus and the Jews. It was not the question whether Jesus did or did not fill certain recognized Jewish positions, such as that of Messiah; it was the question whether grace or legalism represented the truth about God,[47] whether true and final dominion belonged to the Torah or to the Son of man.[48]

2. We return to the title Son of man, which does more than any other to cement the unity of the gospel tradition. We have seen that in the background of this expression both suffering and glory play their part, and that suffering is, broadly speaking, undifferentiated in that it falls upon the people as a whole, while in glory the Son of man represents the people. Suffering is positively evaluated in two ways: in terms of atonement effected by the suffering itself, and in terms of vindication which follows upon the suffering. It is perhaps not unnatural that before the passion, the notion of suffering with the Son of man should be unclearly and variably expressed, and connected mainly with the apocalyptic vindication of the suffering group; and that afterwards, as the Church looked back upon the cross in which one died alone for all, it should make the comment, Christ died for our sins, and in our place.

[47] It is not suggested that Judaism is intrinsically legalistic, still less that Christian thought has never been corrupted by legalism. But there certainly was a marked legalistic development in first-century Judaism which went far beyond mere faithfulness to Torah, and it was against this that Jesus (and Paul) reacted, and on this issue that conflict arose.

[48] See below, pp. 95ff.

3

Christ to come

———◆•••◆———

Whatever view is taken of the historical tradition about Jesus, of his relation to the messiahship, and of the circumstances and meaning of his death, it can hardly be denied that the resurrection marks a watershed of decisive importance. The teaching and activity of Jesus were directed towards a future, which appears to have included his death; did it include also the resurrection, and the founding of the Church? Was the future he envisaged the future that happened in the days, the years, the centuries after the first Easter Day? What sort of continuity, if any, exists between Jesus and the Church? Was his preaching of the kingdom fulfilled or falsified in the Christian mission? Most of the problems of New Testament scholarship were posed by Loisy in a dozen words when he wrote, "Jesus foretold the kingdom, and it was the Church that came."[1] It is a familiar but important fact that whereas the word βασιλεία (kingdom) is one of the most common and characteristic in the gospels, the word ἐκκλησία (Church) occurs in only two passages, both exposed to severe critical doubt and objection. Does this fact suggest that the hopes of Jesus were disappointed? that he looked simply for the supernatural establishing of the kingdom of God in power, and not for the continuing existence, in the conditions of this world, of a human community?

We must begin by considering the gospels as they stand;

[1] A. Loisy, *The Gospel and the Church*, 1903, p. 166.

when we have done this we shall be able to consider how faithfully they represent, and how far they pervert, the teaching of Jesus in this matter.

The plan of the future envisaged by the synoptic evangelists is made clearest by Luke—inevitably, since he alone among the evangelists was to continue his work in a second volume in which the future would be described. If we begin with the story of Acts we shall be able to look back to the gospels to see how it is foretold there. Acts opens with appearances of the risen Jesus, which establish beyond doubt the fact of his resurrection. On the occasion of the last of these appearances Jesus is taken up in a cloud and thus parted from his disciples. At the same time a promise is given that as he has gone so he will come again. The return of Jesus is evidently regarded as the term of the story, though (in the nature of things) it has not arrived at the time when the book is written. After the departure of Jesus, the Holy Spirit is given to the community, first on a single notable general occasion, and subsequently at times of special need, when, for example, disciples are arraigned before authorities of various kinds. When left in peace the disciples meet regularly with one another, for prayer, to share in a common meal, and to practise the duties of love and mutual care. They bear witness to Jesus, and preach the Gospel to both Jews and Gentiles, and thus embark upon the evangelization of the world.

There is not a word in this outline account of what (according to Acts) happened in early Christianity that does not have its counterpart in the gospels, in the form either of prediction or of command. The resurrection itself is foretold on almost every occasion when the passion of the Son of man is predicted. "The Son of man must suffer many things and be rejected by the elders and the chief priests and the scribes, and be killed, and after three days rise up" (Mark 8.31). After rising up he would again be seen by his disciples; this prediction is attested even by Mark (16.7; cf. 14.28), although in this gospel (as it now stands) no resurrection appearances are recorded. The ascension (in the form in which it is narrated in Acts) is not

6

specifically foretold in the gospels, but it is certainly presupposed, especially in the Lucan form of the words of Jesus to
the high priest: "From henceforth the Son of man shall be
seated at the right hand of the power of God" (Luke 22.69).
He could come from earth to heaven, to his place beside God,
only by an ascension of some kind. The Marcan form of the
saying (Mark 14.62), which speaks of the coming of the Son of
man from heaven, equally, if not quite so clearly, assumes an
ascension.[2] There is also material that by-passes the resurrection as an independent incident, and proceeds directly to the
passage of Jesus from earthly to heavenly life. Thus at Mark
14.25 Jesus, with no word about the resurrection, speaks of
drinking wine in the kingdom of God, and at Luke 23.43 he
says to the penitent thief, "To-day you shall be with me in
Paradise". If we may continue to assume the identification of
Jesus with the Son of man (and there is no doubt that the
evangelists made this identification, even if it was not made at
an earlier stage in the tradition), his return with the clouds of
heaven and in great power and glory is predicted. Thus Mark
13.26: "They shall see the Son of man coming in clouds with
great power and glory". The same prediction is affirmed in the
plainest terms by all the evangelists.

The gift of the Spirit on the day of Pentecost is connected in
Acts with the Baptist's prophecy that his greater successor
would perform a baptism with Spirit. The Q version of this
prophecy ("He shall baptize you with Holy Spirit and with
fire": Matt. 3.11; Luke 3.16) is cast in a form which Luke no
doubt saw fulfilled in the external phenomena of the day of
Pentecost (Acts 2.3). The Marcan form (which has no reference
to fire) lacks only this outward circumstance. A general promise
of the gift of the Holy Spirit to all who seek it is given in Luke
11.13, and the special aid of the Spirit is assured to those who
are in special need in Mark 13.11 (and in the parallels, except

---

[2] Some think that the Marcan saying, in its original intention, spoke only
of an ascension to, not of a coming from God; e.g. J. A. T. Robinson,
Jesus and his Coming, 1957, p. 50: "We have here a saying not of visita-
tion from God but of vindication to God."

Luke 21.15, which preserves a more original form[3]): "Do not be anxious what you shall speak, but speak whatever is given you in that hour; for it is not you that speak, but the Holy Spirit."

At the Last Supper, the disciples are bidden to do what Jesus has done (presumably in breaking and distributing bread) "as his memorial" (Luke 22.19), that is, after his death.[4] They are given instruction in prayer, in mutual love, and in humility towards each other. They must not be ashamed of Jesus (Mark 8.38), but bear testimony to him even before their judges (Matt. 10.18; Mark 13.9); the Gospel will be widely proclaimed (Mark 14.9), even to the Gentiles (Mark 13.10).

The parallelism between these predictions and the life of the early Church as it is depicted in Acts is very close, and there are other parts of the gospels that correspond to features of primitive Christian life, as when disciples are warned against persecution, the deceitfulness of riches, or worldly cares (e.g. Mark 4.17,19). In addition to such explicit matters, we have learnt, through form criticism, to see the needs and interests of the Church reflected in many, perhaps all, of the incidents and sayings recorded in the gospels. It is however an important observation that the quantity of explicit prediction of the life of the Church in the time after his death and resurrection that is put into the mouth of Jesus is relatively small. Predictions of the work of the Spirit do, as we have seen, exist, but they are notoriously few. The Gentile mission is hinted at, but only in occasional verses. There is complete silence regarding the structure and form of the Church. The words that prescribe the continuance of the Holy Supper occur in one gospel only, and there in a verse whose authority is textually uncertain.[5] The predictions provide a framework—that is, an interval between

---

[3] See p. 72.

[4] This may not have been the original sense of the words εἰς τὴν ἐμὴν ἀνάμνησιν. See J. Jeremias, *The Eucharistic Words of Jesus*, 1966, pp. 237–55; but also D. R. Jones, "*ANAMNHΣIΣ* in the LXX and the Interpretation of 1 Cor. XI.25*", in *Journal of Theological Studies*, Vol. vi (new series), pp. 183–91.

[5] Luke 22.19b,20 are omitted by important witnesses to the Western Text; the textual state of the whole paragraph is very complicated.

the resurrection and the coming of the Son of man—within which there is room for the Church to exist, but the details are only sketchily filled in.

It is sometimes said that this fact is to the credit of the evangelists as historians: they did not fill their books with *vaticinia ex eventu* referring to matters that were of concern to them though they did not belong to the period of which they were writing. There is substance in this argument, but if it is to be used at all it must be taken a step further. It is certainly true that the gospels contain little *direct* reference to the period after the resurrection; this reflects creditably upon the veracity of the evangelists; therefore we must conclude that Jesus had little to say, and was but little concerned, with this period. This moderate conclusion seems to me beyond dispute; it can however be sharpened further.

When critically studied, most of the references to the future that I have so far mentioned or alluded to fade out of the picture. For example, I have examined elsewhere all the references to the Holy Spirit,[6] and there is perhaps not one that can be accepted as belonging to the earliest stratum of tradition. The Baptist predicted a future baptism not with the Holy Spirit, but with wind and fire, the elements of judgement. Jesus said that the Father would give good things (Matt. 7.11) to those who asked; the Holy Spirit is a Lucan estimate of what "good things" might mean. The earliest form of the promise of divine assistance to disciples on trial spoke not of the Holy Spirit but of a "mouth and wisdom which none of your adversaries shall be able to withstand or gainsay" (Luke 21.15). Similar observations can be made with regard to the few gospel references to a mission among the Gentiles. There is no need to review the evidence here, for it has been fully discussed by Joachim Jeremias, who concludes "that Jesus limited his activity to Israel, and imposed the same limitation upon his disciples".[7] It is evident that instructions about the mutual

---

[6] *The Holy Spirit and the Gospel Tradition*, 1947; new edition, 1966.
[7] J. Jeremias, *Jesus' Promise to the Nations*, Studies in Biblical Theology, 24, 1958, p. 55.

relations of charity and forbearance that ought to exist between the disciples do not refer to any particular time; the disciples needed this kind of teaching during the ministry at least as much as they did afterwards. The same applies to teaching about prayer.

Thus the question is raised whether in the earliest strata of the gospel tradition, and in the teaching of Jesus himself, the continuing existence of a historical community is contemplated. It is no answer to this question to say that the moral and eschatological teaching of Jesus implies a community, practising the duties of love and looking for the coming of the Son of man; this implication is satisfied already before his death and resurrection, and we have to inquire whether the outlook of Jesus into the future left any interval after his passion for such a community to continue to exist. It is certain that the question cannot be answered by reference to verses in which the word ἐκκλησία (Church) occurs. In Matthew 18.17 we are in the midst of a passage which shows clearly[8] the traces of cross-currents in later Christian thought and practice—how is the Church's duty to keep itself pure to be balanced against its duty to love and succour the offender and the outcast? In "Tell it to the Church" we have a saying whose setting is that not of the ministry of Jesus but of the settled life of an established community. At Matthew 16.18 the conclusion of many years of dispute is probably this, that if the word ἐκκλησία refers to a community in this age the authenticity of the saying cannot be maintained; it can be maintained only if by the word ἐκκλησία Jesus referred to a supernatural and apocalyptic body belonging to the time of the end. In either case the verse falls out of consideration.

We have already seen that the gospels as they stand do look forward to an interval between the resurrection and the coming of the Son of man—inevitably so, since they were written within this interval. We have to inquire whether the time-scheme that was forced upon the evangelists by the unrelenting course of

[8] See G. Barth, in G. Bornkamm, G. Barth, and H. J. Held, *Tradition and Interpretation in Matthew*, 1963, p. 84.

events was shared by Jesus himself, and this is a delicate inquiry, because it was inevitable that his utterances, whatever they may originally have been, should be, if not consciously altered, at least understood and reinterpreted in the light of passing years. It may fairly be said that any sayings ascribed to Jesus which agree with the evangelists' viewpoint will have to be looked at with some suspicion, and that special attention ought to be given to any which appear to disagree.

Among modern critical scholars who have argued that Jesus himself did look for an interval between his resurrection and the *parousia*, within which the historic existence of the Church falls, two outstanding names are G. R. Beasley-Murray[9] and W. G. Kümmel.[10] It will be well to note their arguments. The main weight of the case rests on passages which speak of suffering as in store for the disciples. Dr Beasley-Murray cites the following: Luke 12.11f.; Mark 10.38f.; Luke 12.51f.; Matthew 5.10f.; Luke 12.4f., 9; Mark 8.35. Some of these passages, notably perhaps Matthew 5.10f., do seem to bear witness to the persecution of the Church after the resurrection. But, as I have already pointed out, this is in no way surprising. The evangelists wrote in a time of persecution, and it would have been astonishing if, in sayings of Jesus that referred to suffering, they had not seen a forecast of what they and their contemporaries were experiencing. We must however recall that there is good evidence that, at least at some stages of his ministry and under some aspects of his thought, Jesus expected his disciples to suffer with him, that is, to suffer when he suffered. The evangelists knew that this had not happened, and it was inevitable that in editing this material they should make it square with what they knew to be the facts. The process may have been conscious or unconscious, or sometimes one and sometimes the other; in any case, it is not possible to use these predictions of suffering for the Church as evidence that Jesus looked forward to a period of Church life beyond his death and resurrection.

9 *Jesus and the Future*, 1954; *A Commentary on Mark Thirteen*, 1957.
10 *Promise and Fulfilment*, Studies in Biblical Theology, 23, 1957.

Another passage cited by Dr Beasley-Murray is Mark 13.10
(to which may be added Mark 14.9). There is no reason to
doubt that Mark understood both these prophecies in terms of
the task of world evangelization, a task in which he himself,
with his fellow-Christians, was engaged. But it has to be
demonstrated not only that these sayings go back to Jesus but
also that their original meaning was that attached to them by
Mark. Dr Jeremias has made it seem probable that their
original sense was different: Mark 14.9 "did not originally
refer to a worldwide mission of the disciples, but to the final
fulfilment and the last judgement ... a similar interpretation
should be given to the closely-related isolated saying in Mark
13.10. ... Here, too, the original reference is not to human
proclamation, but to an apocalyptic event, namely, the
angelic proclamation of God's final act (cf. Rev. 14.6f.)".[11]

To the passages brought to bear on the subject by Dr Beasley-
Murray, Dr Kümmel adds the following: Mark 2.18ff.; 14.25,28;
Matthew 23.38f. In the little parable of the wedding the
crucial verse is Mark 2.20, and on this verse considerable
critical doubt must rest. Verses 18, 19 are best understood as
simple similitude, justifying the behaviour of the disciples: you
can no more expect them to fast than guests at a wedding. In
the ministry of Jesus men do not seek to force God to act by the
melancholy practices of religion, but rejoice that he has already
acted. The next verse however makes a leap into allegory; Jesus
is identified with the Bridegroom-Messiah, he predicts his
passion in public, and the Church's practice of fasting[12] is
justified. The saying is rightly described by Dr Jeremias as
Gemeindebildung[13] and Dr Kümmel's defence of verse 19b, and
its implication that there will be a time when the disciples are
not accompanied by the Bridegroom is not convincing. Verses
18, 19a are complete in themselves and do not call for a supplement.[14] The sayings at the Supper (and Luke 22.16,18 are

---

11 *Jesus' Promise* (see above, n. 7), pp. 22f.

12 Cf. Didache 8.1.

13 J. Jeremias, *The Parables of Jesus*, 1963, p. 52; also *Theologisches
Wörterbuch zum Neuen Testament*, Vol. IV, p. 1096.

14 Cf. Kümmel, op. cit. pp. 75ff.

at least as significant as their Marcan counterparts) do, as Dr Kümmel says, presuppose a time of affliction before the coming of the kingdom of God; but how near the affliction was! There is no need to seek it beyond the resurrection. Only Matt. 23.38f. remains. This is a Q saying, and all that need be said about it here is that Matthew and Luke place it in completely different settings. In Matthew it does appear to refer to a period between the death of Jesus and his glorious return, during which Jerusalem is devastated and lies in ruins; in Luke it does not. Probably each evangelist has prepared his own setting for the saying, and this means that the meaning given to it in Matthew must be regarded as editorial.

It cannot (in my opinion) be said that a case has been made out for the view that Jesus looked forward to an interval between his death and resurrection on the one hand, and, on the other, the establishing of the kingdom of God in power, or the coming of the Son of man. Indeed, Dr Beasley-Murray and Dr Kümmel seem to get the worst of both worlds, for though they find room in Jesus' thought for an interval before the *parousia* they believe that he expected this interval to last no more than a generation, so that even on their view the accuracy of Jesus' forecast is not saved.

This, however, is no place at which to leave the matter. Even if the gospels as they stand give us an inaccurate account of the way in which the future presented itself to the mind of Jesus, we should not conclude that he made no reference to the future at all. The development of the tradition, of which I shall say more later, is more intelligible if it had a definite starting-point, even though it may have diverged from it. Moreover, if the argument of the second lecture was correct, and Jesus did (in forms now not fully recoverable) predict and interpret his approaching passion, the interpretation must have included the prediction of some kind of vindication beyond the passion. It is inconceivable that Jesus simply predicted the complete and final failure of his mission. It is highly probable, indeed, that New Testament students since Albert Schweitzer and Johannes Weiss have been right in seeing in the teaching of Jesus a strong eschatological and apocalyptic element.[15] But, if Jesus did predict not only his death but also some kind of supernatural vindication to follow it, what form did he believe that the vindication would take?

At this point we must take up again the Son of man sayings A number of these refer to the ministry of Jesus on earth, both in its authority (for he forgives sins and rules over the Sabbath) and in its humiliation (for he has nowhere to lay his head). Other sayings point to his suffering and death; almost though not quite all of these go on to speak of his resurrection. In Matthew and Luke this is predicted for the "third day", but this dating is evidently a correction of the surprising Marcan phrase, "after three days"—surprising, for these words give an inaccurate description of the interval between Friday and Sunday, which Mark himself, like the other evangelists, takes to be the interval between Jesus' death and resurrection. It was allowed to stand in Mark (though not without textual variations) presumably because it could be taken to mean "a short time",[16] but it is very improbable that it was made up on the basis of known historical events, as these are described not only in the gospels but, much earlier, in 1 Corinthians 15.4. Knowledge of the historical circumstances of the trial and execution of Jesus had already begun to work upon the predictions, and it is probable that knowledge of the resurrection as an event had done so too, before (as well as after) they reached Mark, but the Marcan predictions of the resurrection represent a relatively early stage in this development, and we may be fairly confident that it was foretold that some kind of vindicating event would happen "after three days"—that is, very soon after the crucifixion. Since, at the latest, the time of Daniel 12.2, the idea of resurrection had been known in Judaism, and it was precisely in the context of vindication (rather than that of philosophical speculation about future life) that the idea became

[15] See however n. 13 on p. 8.
[16] Cf. Hosea 6.2: ὑγιάσει ἡμᾶς μετὰ δύο ἡμέρας, ἐν τῇ ἡμέρᾳ τῇ τρίτῃ ἀναστησόμεθα (after two days he will heal us, on the third day we shall rise up).

familiar.[17] Those who had given their service and their lives for the national religion would not lose their reward on account of the very loyalty that had led to their death before the dawn of the new age. Daniel 12.2 looks on this collectively: the saints would rise to take part in the bliss God had prepared for his people; the same conviction that vindication would follow upon suffering is expressed more individualistically by the seven brothers in 2 Maccabees 7, who are as certain that there will be no resurrection for their tormentors as that they will themselves be raised up. The fourth brother speaks for them all: "We must choose to die at the hands of men and look forward to the God-given hope of being raised up again by him; but for you there shall be no resurrection to life" (2 Macc. 7.14). That Jesus should similarly predict that, after dying in fulfilment of the commission laid upon him by God, he would be vindicated, and that he should give his vindication the form of resurrection, is thus in no way surprising. He would suffer and die, but God would not leave him in corruption; when he had done God's work God would show his approval and acceptance by raising him from the dead, and that soon. We may compare the prayer of the youngest of the seven brothers, that God would intervene on behalf of his people speedily (ταχύ, 2 Macc. 7.37). There is no need to suppose that Jesus always expressed this hope of resurrection in individual terms. Just as he appears to have predicted (at least on some occasions) that his disciples would suffer with him, so he will have predicted that they would share his resurrection. The resurrection is in fact the inaugural act of the new age, which only those who survived to see it, and those who were raised from death for the purpose, would experience.

In another group of sayings it is predicted that the Son of man will come with glory in the clouds of heaven, accompanied by the heavenly hosts. With these may be classed Luke 22.69, which states that the Son of man will be seated on the right hand of the power of God; that is, it states that he will be in heaven, a glorious and vindicated figure (vindicated, whether

---

[17] Cf. N. H. Snaith, "Justice and Immortality", in *Scottish Journal of Theology*, 17, pp. 309–24.

his vindication is generally visible, as in a *parousia*, or not). Some would class Mark 14.62 with Luke 22.69, denying that it speaks of a coming of the Son of man to earth, but in Mark the sequence (seated, and coming) seems decisive;[18] the Son of man will be exalted to heaven and thereby vindicated; later his vindication will be manifested, and he will carry out his apocalyptic role, when he comes from heaven to earth.

Some passages simply predict the coming in glory of the Son of man, and do not bring this glorious *parousia* into direct relation with any earlier record of expectation of suffering and death. Such is, or appears to be, Mark 13.26, where Jesus declares, "Then they shall see the Son of man coming in clouds with great power and glory". If these passages stood alone it would be natural to suppose that Jesus was speaking of a person other than himself; that he was a messianic prophet, like Daniel, himself a suffering witness for the true faith but pointing forward to the vindication of the people of God by (or, in) a supernatural agent. It is not true, however, though this is sometimes said,[19] that prophecies of the *parousia* of the Son of man are never brought into relation with prophecies of suffering. This relation is sometimes made. An outstanding example is Mark 8.38, which we have already considered in another connection. This verse undoubtedly has in mind the suffering of Jesus (and in the same context—Mark 8.31—this is spoken of as the suffering of the Son of man), and asserts that it is men's attitude to the suffering and reproach of Jesus that will determine the attitude to them of the glorious Son of man. It is implied that the coming of the Son of man will mean the vindication of the suffering and humiliated Jesus, and at the same time the vindication of those who are prepared to share his earthly lot. Collective suffering, and also collective vindication, are in mind, though a pre-eminent part is played by Jesus in the one and by the Son of man in the other. The fact that this saying

---

[18] Against Robinson, see n. 2 above.

[19] The sharp threefold division of Son of man sayings is made by scholars as diverse as R. Bultmann (e.g. *Theologie des Neuen Testaments*, 1948–53, p. 31) and V. Taylor (e.g. *The Names of Jesus*, 1953, pp. 30–5).

appears to distinguish between the historical Jesus and the future Son of man proves its antiquity. The tradition undoubtedly came to identify Jesus with the Son of man, but it had not yet reached the stage of clarifying Mark 8.38 (compare p. 32).

The same point is made by the Q saying of Matthew 19.28 = Luke 22.28–30. When the two forms of the saying are compared it appears that both have undergone editorial modification, the Matthean less than the Lucan. The use in Luke of the verb διατίθεμαι, to make a covenant, is probably due to the context in which Luke has placed the saying (cf. v. 20). πειρασμός, trial, is a Lucan word (six times; in Matthew twice, in Mark once), and may have been suggested by the nearness (in Luke, not in Matthew) of the Gethsemane story (cf. vv. 40, 46). The image of eating and drinking at Jesus' table which occurs in Luke is probably due to the fact that Luke has placed the saying in the context of the Supper. The term Son of man occurs only in Matthew, but since Luke has so considerably modified the saying in the light of the context in which he has placed it it is reasonably probable that he omitted "Son of man" rather than that Matthew inserted it.[20] The point is in the end not important, since if "Son of man" was not used Jesus was speaking all the more plainly of his own future vindication. In the Matthean context (cf. v. 27) ὑμεῖς οἱ ἀκολουθήσαντές μοι means, "You who have followed me in my earthly sufferings, so as to share them". For such men, the glory and reign of the Son of man (or of Jesus himself) will mean glory and authority in the renewed people of God in the age to come.

Another verse that even more directly connects the glorious coming of the Son of man with his earlier suffering is Luke 17.25. This is often treated as a secondary element in the tradition, and so it may well be; even if however Luke has constructed it on the basis of such passages as Mark 8.31 it remains significant that he has placed it here, along with more general references to suffering.

[20] Though Matthew does occasionally (e.g. at 16.13) insert "Son of man" into Marcan contexts that did not contain it.

Less immediately relevant but of considerable importance is Matthew 10.23. This occurs in the Matthean charge to the apostles. They will incur punishments and sufferings of many kinds; they will be hated by all men for Jesus' name. They must hasten on from city to city, not lingering in the forlorn hope of turning persecution into a welcome, for however quickly they move they will not have completed the cities of Israel before the coming of the Son of man. This is the end (τέλος, v. 22), which will bring salvation to those who have endured suffering. There is nothing here about the suffering of Jesus, or of the Son of man; but the context is determined by the apocalyptic suffering of the disciples of Jesus, and the coming of the Son of man. Other passages show that the suffering of disciples cannot be completely separated from the suffering of their master. This passage thus has a particular interest of its own, and also completes the list of gospel sources, for we now have material from Mark, Q, L, and M.

Similar reasoning,[21] however, will show that Mark 13.26 (cited above as apparently an example of the "pure" eschatological glory of the Son of man) should be included here. The coming of the Son of man takes place "after that affliction" (13.24), and is followed by the mission of the angels, who will gather together the elect (13.27), who will have escaped so narrowly from suffering (13.20) and from deception (13.22). The coming of the Son of man is the vindication and deliverance of the suffering righteous, though in the context the "righteous" are the elect in general, and there is no reference to the suffering of Jesus.

Thus the sayings that speak of the glory of the Son of man are not so completely detached from the theme of suffering as is often supposed; in truth, they are closely connected with it. They do however form a group distinct from those that predict the resurrection of the Son of man. What we never find is a statement in the form: "After his suffering the Son of man will be vindicated by being raised from the dead; later he will come

---

[21] It was pointed out on p. 52 (n. 30) that there is a significant body of material common to Matthew 10 and Mark 13.

in glory with the clouds of heaven". Indeed, when the proposition is stated in this form it is evident that it needs a middle term dealing with the ascension of the Son of man; and, unless we are to find it in Luke 22.69 (significantly in the first volume of Luke-Acts), there is no such term explicit in the gospels. This means that sayings about the *parousia* of the Son of man, though in the gospels they now refer to the event which will bring to an end the Church's history of witness and mission, must originally have served a quite different purpose; that is, they were another form, alternative to the resurrection sayings, of expressing the conviction that the Son of man would be vindicated.

At first sight, this conclusion seems to suggest that the *parousia* sayings were the point at which the theology of the primitive Church entered the tradition.[22] The heavenly Lord was identified with the apocalyptic Son of man; predictions of his coming in this role were read back into the story of Jesus, and gradually the title Son of man was pressed back to the resurrection, the passion, and the earthly life. I do not think this is a necessary conclusion. There is no reason why Jesus should not have expressed his convictions in regard to the future in both ways, using the language both of resurrection and of *parousia*. As I have said, if he could not count on vindication of some kind he must have drawn the conclusion that his work was being rejected by God, and the obvious and proper course would have been to withdraw from a conflict that would be not only unequal and unpleasant, but actually sinful, because God did not will it and would not support it. It is evident that he believed himself to be doing the will of God in continuing his ministry to the outcast and in declaring God's forgiveness and his claim upon men; why should he have been less confident of resurrection than the seven brothers in 2 Maccabees 7, less confident of heavenly intervention than Daniel? The question whether he identified himself with the Son of man, though not unimportant, is at this stage irrelevant;

[22] See the Excursus in H. E. Tödt, *The Son of Man in the Synoptic Tradition*, 1965, pp. 329–47.

the glory of the Son of man would be his vindication, whether he himself was the Son of man or not.

If Jesus spoke of his vindication in eschatological terms, sometimes as resurrection, sometimes as the glory of the Son of man, the tradition of his words was exposed to inevitable modification when, on the first Easter Day, the disciples became convinced that Jesus was no longer dead but was again with them, and embarked upon a period which they believed was to be terminated by his return from heaven. The two forms of prediction were now carefully distinguished. Resurrection "after a short time" became in due course (as early as I Cor. 15.4) resurrection "on the third day", and the glorious coming of the Son of man was left over as a reappearance of Jesus to bring his disciples' work to a close.

Can we discover when Jesus himself believed that his vindication would take place? Two preliminary points may be borne in mind here.

1. In Mark the resurrection is announced as taking place "after three days". As we have seen,[23] this note of time was not based on the event as it actually took place (on the third day); the words mean simply "after a short time". Probably therefore Jesus did not specify the interval between his death and vindication; but he did not expect it to be long.

2. The early Church expected the *parousia* to take place within the first generation of Christians. For our purpose it is less important that Paul held this belief than that it appears in the gospel tradition. It is impossible to make Mark 13 mean anything less than that Christians contemporary with Mark believed that they would see the whole story through up to the coming of the Son of man. Mark 13.30 alone is decisive, unless strained meanings are to be given to either γενεά (generation) or ταῦτα πάντα (all these things), and this verse is not contradicted by 13.32, which states that within the general nearness of the end no one can name the precise moment of its arrival.

[23] See p. 77.

The hearers of the discourse are encouraged to endure to the end, notwithstanding the universal hatred they will incur for Jesus' sake (v. 13). They will see (ὅταν ἴδητε, when you see, second person plural) the abomination of desolation standing where he ought not (v. 14). The Lord has shortened the days of suffering so that the elect may survive (v. 20). The hearers of the discourse will see the signs of the end (v. 29, ὅταν ἴδητε, when you see, again), and will be able to deduce from them that it (or the Son of man?)[24] is already at their doors. This early dating of the end became a source of embarrassment, and, especially in the later gospels, traces appear of editorial and theological steps taken in view of the "delay of the *parousia*"; it is most improbable that the Church created this embarrassment for itself, and probable therefore that the conviction that the vindicating *parousia* would happen soon has deep roots in the tradition.

These preliminary observations suggest an early date for the event of vindication. This conclusion can be confirmed by a further argument. I have already noted[25] that, though the sayings about the Son of man and the sayings about the kingdom of God are not combined, they run parallel to each other; it is therefore significant for our purpose that Jesus seems to have expected that the kingdom of God would come in power very shortly. This is plainly stated in Mark 9.1 (which in Matthew 16.28 is made to refer to the coming of the Son of man—a secondary alteration, but one that shows how closely Matthew connected the two themes). It is true that this verse contains numerous exegetical problems. The perfect participle ἐληλυθυῖαν (having come) has been taken[26] to mean that the coming of the kingdom in power precedes the promise that men will see it, that is, to mean that the coming has already taken place during the ministry of Jesus. This is not however required by

---

[24] In Mark 13.29 no subject is expressed for ἐγγύς ἐστιν. Matthew (24.33) follows Mark; Luke (21.31) supplies ἡ βασιλεία τοῦ θεοῦ.

[25] See pp. 30f.

[26] Notably by C. H. Dodd, *The Parables of the Kingdom*, 1936, pp. 53f. The point has been frequently debated in the last thirty years.

the grammar, and other material in the gospels, especially the parables based on the growth of seeds, suggests that, during the ministry, the kingdom, so far as it is present at all, is present only in germ. A different kind of problem is raised by the fact that none of those present did survive to see the coming of the kingdom in power, if this is to be interpreted in apocalyptic terms, as Matthew's reference to the coming of the Son of man suggests. For this reason it has been suggested that the coming of the kingdom should be interpreted otherwise, as the transfiguration, the resurrection, or the gift of the Spirit on the day of Pentecost. None of these suggestions in plausible. It may be that Mark himself thought of the transfiguration as the fulfilment of the promise, and that it was for this reason that he introduced his note of time in 9.2. But the suggestion, even if Mark made it, is impossible: if Jesus solemnly affirmed that some at least of his hearers would survive his prediction by one week he was uttering ridiculous bathos. The earlier strata of the tradition show no interest in the Holy Spirit, so that we must rule out the suggestion that Jesus was referring to the events of Pentecost (Acts 2). That the resurrection should be intended is not too far from the truth, if we are right in thinking that the resurrection was one of the forms in which Jesus expressed the vindication to which he looked forward. But there is no indication that if the resurrection was in mind it was thought of as an interim event. If the coming of the kingdom in power is to be identified with the resurrection, then the resurrection must be taken to be the comprehensive consummation of the eschatological process which Jesus' ministry had inaugurated, not as an event such as that recorded in the gospels.

We may safely leave some loose ends in the discussion of this passage, for we have already established the relevant conclusion. Mark 9.1 adds to the evidence that Jesus expected the vindication of his work to come at no distant date. The statement that some, but presumably not all, of his hearers would live to see it, though it excludes an interpretation in terms of the transfiguration, does not exclude but requires an early date. The context (Mark 8.35–8) shows that circumstances were

7

envisaged in which disciples of Jesus would have many opportunities of dying otherwise than by senility. This passage too helps to bring together the themes of suffering and vindication.

It seems then that the earliest strata of the tradition represent Jesus as foreseeing his death (at least, the probability of it), and fitting it into God's eschatological purpose by the conviction that it would be speedily followed by a divine act of vindication coincident with, perhaps part of, the consummation of the kingdom of God and its establishing in power. So far as the vindication touched him personally it might be expressed as resurrection, or as the glory of the Son of man, both apocalyptic notions with which he and his hearers were familiar. This conclusion is consistent with three notable facts observed in Lecture 2. I pointed out there[27] (a) that the Last Supper was held in the setting of a fervent hope for the appearance of the Messiah and the speedy establishing of the kingdom of God; (b) that in the garden of Gethsemane Jesus prayed that he might be spared the cup of suffering, that is, that the vindication of his work might anticipate his death; and (c) that Jesus died with words of disappointment on his lips: God had deserted him, and failed to vindicate him, even in the moment of death; his work was in vain.

Putting together the observations that have now been made, it is difficult to doubt that Jesus had expected that his ministry would culminate in the eschatological affliction, and that his vindication would follow immediately upon, or even interrupt, his ministry and suffering, and difficult to think that his prediction had taken the form that it has in the gospels as they now stand, where it can be summed up as death—delay—resurrection—delay—return; and the fact that the disciples seem to have had no idea that this would be the course of events confirms our conclusion. Luke 24.21 ("We were hoping—$\eta\lambda\pi i\zeta o\mu\epsilon\nu$—that he was the one who would redeem Israel") can scarcely be taken as the actual words of disciples uttered on the first Easter Day, but it probably represents fairly enough their attitude after the

[27] See pp. 46ff.

crucifixion. They were disappointed, and they were not expecting a resurrection—though, as soon as the resurrection happened, they were able to draw on their recollection of what Jesus had foretold, and immediately to begin the process of sorting out the material into patterns that fitted the actual course of history.

This simple observation brings us to the central point in the present lecture, and to the crux of the modern discussion of the Jesus of history. We know that we cannot write a biography of Jesus; but we also know that we are not completely ignorant of what he taught and what he did. Our difficulty arises not out of the fact that we know next to nothing about Jesus, but out of the content of what we do know when this is viewed in relation to the Church and the Church's preaching of its heavenly Lord. Again, we know of the Church that it looked back to the resurrection as the foundation of its life, mission, and doctrine, and as the beginning of its history; but we also know that, though the resurrection experience is a historically verifiable event, the resurrection (as the New Testament understands it) in the nature of things is not; moreover, we have now seen that Jesus did not himself predict this kind of interim vindication of his work, though he did predict that his work would be vindicated. The question inevitably arises whether the Church can be regarded as a legitimate continuation of the work of Jesus; or, to put the matter in another way, more directly related to our theme, whether the Church was justified in using the historical tradition about Jesus as it did. If the historical Jesus did not claim to be Messiah and Son of God, these terms being written into the tradition (not without some basis) in the course of its transmission, if Jesus' view of his approaching suffering was contingent (in that he was not at all times sure of its necessity), and to some extent communal, and if beyond the time of suffering he envisaged no period of continuing history, in which a Church organized in this world might find a place, but an apocalyptic act of vindication—if, that is, the conclusions we have reached so far are even approximately true, what historical justification remains for a preaching such as Paul sums up in the words (1 Cor. 15.3ff.), "Christ died for our sins according to the Scriptures, and was buried, and was raised on the third day according to the Scriptures, and appeared to" various witnesses? This is the problem of the historical Jesus; though it might be better to call it the historical problem of the *kerygma*.

I have stated the question sharply, and the sharpness is both justified and helpful to the student; but it would be a great mistake to suppose that the resurrection presented itself to the disciples as in any sense a problem. It was taken immediately as a partial vindication of Jesus, shortly to be completed in the coming of the Son of man, and it was the historical Jesus who was vindicated. He who had engaged in controversy with Pharisees and scribes had now been shown to be right; he who had been put to death by the concerted action of Jewish and Roman authorities was now proved to have been the innocent victim of ignorance and malice (cf. Acts 2.36; 3.13f.,17; 4.10,27; 5.28,30). His claim to authority within the people of God was justified, and his disciples could look upon themselves as more truly the people of God than the civil and religious leaders, and the pietistic groups, within Israel. It is true that the vindication had not fallen out in the way in which the historical Jesus had expected it, and inevitably therefore the figure of Jesus was from the beginning subject to reinterpretation and distortion; but it was a genuinely historical figure that was being viewed through the refracting medium of the resurrection faith. Of this the clearest evidence is provided by the features which escaped reinterpretation and enable us to reconstruct some features of the actual life and teaching of Jesus. In the early stages, the process of reinterpretation must have been almost entirely unconscious; of this the remodelling of the predictions of vindication is the most important example.

The vindication was the vindication of the historical Jesus. A parallel fact, equally simple and important, is that the group that found itself living in the post-resurrection epoch, that is, in a period that partially anticipated the age to come, was the same group that had accompanied Jesus during his earlier ministry. The vindication of the historical Jesus was at the same time the rehabilitation of the historical group of disciples. That which became the Church had been in existence, though not as the Church, in the earlier period with which the gospel story deals, and those who first reinterpreted the tradition had a place within the tradition itself.

The matter cannot, however, be left here. If an attempt is made to trace the history through from the story of Jesus to that of the primitive Church, a complex mixture of continuity and discontinuity appears, and we must disentangle the threads as well as we can. The best procedure will be to return to the gospel sayings about the Son of man. In the tradition as we have it, these sayings, better than any other group, provide continuity through the whole stretch of history with which we are concerned. The Son of man lives an earthly life, eating and drinking (Matt. 11.19; Luke 7.34), the friend, and the saviour, of publicans and sinners (ibid.; Luke 19.10), though he has no settled home (Matt. 8.20; Luke 9.58). He has authority over the Sabbath (Mark 2.28), and to forgive sins (Mark 2.10). At the end of this earthly career, he suffers: delivered up by his own people into the hands of sinners, he is mocked, scourged, and crucified. After his sufferings he rises from the dead (Mark 8.31; etc.). The Son of man also dwells in glory (Luke 22.69), and will come from this glory to take part in judgement, it may be as witness and counsel, or as judge (Mark 13.26; etc.).

But to make such a collection of passages is only to state what we have to prove. We can do more. On the basis of studies we have already made[28] we can claim, independently of these gospel sayings, that the Son of man figure is in himself bound up with the idea of suffering (and suffering embraces both an earthly life and an earthly death), and equally with the idea of heavenly glory. So much stands firm in non-Christian sources, though the apocalypses, absorbed by the prospect of future glory, tend to exclude the element of suffering. This being so we must inquire whether it is conceivable that Jesus combined

[28] See pp. 41–5.

these views of the Son of man with each other, and whether he attached both to himself. If so, we shall have achieved, not indeed direct continuity between Jesus and the post-resurrection Church, but at least some ground on which such continuity might stand.

Substantial difficulties remain. How can suffering and glory be combined in one figure? Did Jesus in fact forecast his own suffering and glory? Did he, a human being, identify himself with the heavenly Son of man? In addition to these questions, there is the doubt that besets every occurrence of the title "Son of man"; did this belong to the apocalyptic thinking of the early Church, and was it read back into the gospel story as a Christological expedient designed to explain the figure of Jesus? Some of these questions have already been considered, but a little more work remains to be done on the background.

So far, in speaking of the background of the Son of man figure I have confined myself to Daniel. It is now time to turn also to the Ethiopic book of Enoch.[29] In the central section of this book (the so-called Similitudes, chapters 37–71) a figure described as the (or that) Son of man appears with some frequency. He is an apocalyptic figure, appearing in or from heaven to execute eschatological functions. He is himself the Elect and Righteous One, and he comes to avenge the elect and righteous upon their oppressors. He thus stands in some kind of representative relationship to the people of God, or at least to the righteous remnant of the people.

> And there I saw One, who had a head of days,
> And his head was white like wool,
> And with him was another being whose countenance had the appearance of a man,
> And his face was full of graciousness, like one of the holy angels.
>
> .   .   .   .
>
> This is the Son of man who hath righteousness,
> With whom dwelleth righteousness,

---

[29] The quotations from Enoch (with the signs of supposed corruption and interpolation) are from R. H. Charles's translation, except 71.14 (p. 91).

And who revealeth all the treasures of that which is hidden,
Because the Lord of Spirits hath chosen him,
And whose lot hath the pre-eminence before the Lord of Spirits
    in uprightness for ever.
And this Son of man whom thou hast seen
Shall † raise up † the kings and the mighty from their seats,
[And the strong from their thrones],
And shall loosen the reins of the strong,
And break the teeth of the sinners (46.1–4).

There is a similar passage in chapter 62, which also adds the
positive side:

And the righteous and elect shall be saved on that day,
And they shall never thenceforward see the face of the sinners and
    unrighteous.
And the Lord of Spirits will abide over them,
And with that Son of man shall they eat
And lie down and rise up for ever and ever (62.13f.).

Thus the Son of man is pre-existent, in that he has been hidden
in the presence of God before the unfolding of human history,
but he appears in action only at the end of time. We do however
catch a glimpse of him before this. In this apocalypse it is
Enoch (Gen. 5.18–24) who receives the revelation about the
Son of man and learns the secret of the future. At the end of the
Similitudes however (but before the beginning of the apocalyptic story they disclose) Enoch is taken up to heaven, and
is there informed of the extraordinary truth that he himself is
the Son of man.

And it came to pass after this that my spirit was translated,
And it ascended into the heavens . . .

.   .   .   .

And he came to me and greeted me with his voice and said unto
    me,
Thou art the Son of man who is born unto righteousness;
And righteousness abides over thee,
And the righteousness of the Head of Days forsakes thee not.
                                    (71.1,14).

It is not surprising that R. H. Charles, in his great edition of
Enoch,[30] regarded the text as at this point corrupt, and felt it

30 R. H. Charles, *The Book of Enoch*, 1912.

necessary to change the second person singular into the third person. Enoch (according to Charles's emendation) was not told "Thou art the Son of man", but had the Son of man pointed out to him: "This is the Son of man". Charles was undoubtedly right in claiming that the text as it stands does not make sense. At least, it does not make what a modern western reader would regard as sense. The Son of man has existed from before creation in heaven. During 365 years (according to Gen. 5.23) of this eternity, the man Enoch lived a distinct human life on earth. It is not reasonable that when, at the end of these 365 years, Enoch is translated to heaven he should be told that he is another person, of a different order of being. But reasonable or not, this appears to be what the author wrote.

For this conclusion it is a not inconsiderable argument that the reading of the manuscripts is, "Thou art the Son of man". We owe the manuscript tradition of Enoch mainly to Christians, who would have been much more likely to remove than to create an identification of the Son of man with Enoch. But there is a further argument, of great weight. It is probable that the author of Enoch, in speaking of the patriarch's ascension and identification with the Son of man, was simply interpreting what he understood to be the meaning of the book of Daniel (which he certainly knew and used).

In study of the "Son of man" it is customary to concentrate attention on Daniel 7.13, the vision of one "like a son of man" (כבר אנש), who comes with the clouds of heaven. That this use of the expression stands by itself is apparent to the critical reader, but it will not necessarily have been so evident to the kind of man who wrote 1 Enoch. It will be remembered that Daniel 7 is in Aramaic; chapters 8—12 are in Hebrew, and identity of terminology cannot therefore be expected, but there are in the closing chapters of the book several phrases that recall 7.13; thus

8.15: כמראה גבר = ὡς ὅρασις ἀνθρώπου (as the appearance of a man)

10.16: ‎כדמות בני אדם‎ = (Theodotion) ὡς ὁμοίωσις υἱοῦ (but LXX
reads χειρὸς for υἱοῦ) ἀνθρώπου (as the likeness of a son
(LXX, hand) of man)

10.18: ‎כמראה אדם‎ = ὡς ὅρασις ἀνθρώπου (as the appearance of a
man)

Angels are described by the word *man:* 8.16 (‎אדם‎, ἄνθρωπος);
9.21 (‎איש‎, ἀνήρ); 10.5; 12.6,7 (a man clothed in linen, ‎איש‎,
ἄνθρωπος). In addition, Daniel himself is addressed as "Son of
man" in 8.17 (‎בן אדם‎, υἱὲ ἀνθρώπου), and as a man specially
beloved by God in 10.11,19 (‎איש חמדות‎, ἄνθρωπος ἐλεεινός; in
Theodotion, ἀνὴρ ἐπιθυμιῶν). Thus Daniel, who receives visions
and writes about a Son of man, is addressed as Son of man. The
Enochic identification of the recipient of revelation with the
heavenly Son of man may not have been directly and ex-
clusively due to exegesis of these passages,[31] but there can be
little doubt that the author thought of himself as writing in
harmony with his Scriptural source. Nor indeed was he completely mistaken in this, for though our own historical exegesis
of Daniel will rightly distinguish the quasi-historical legends
about Daniel and his colleagues at the Babylonian court, and
the mythological, probably non-Jewish, sources of the later
chapters, and will place the editing of both in the known
historical circumstances of the period of oppression under
Antiochus Epiphanes, the simple reader of Daniel at the beginning of the Christian era certainly did not approach the book
in this way. For him, Daniel (like Enoch) was a historical person
who represented the Jews, and remained faithful at a time of
trial. As faithful confessor he received comforting revelations
of the end, including a vision of a figure who looked like man
as God made him, and received on behalf of God's people their
rightful dominion and sovereignty. If Daniel, the representative
of God's people, who wrote of this "Son of man" who was also
the representative of God's people, is in addition addressed as
"Son of man", how should one not identify the two figures?
That Daniel was busy interpreting dreams and dealing with

[31] Professor K. Koch, of Hamburg, pointed out to me that the fact that
the prophet Ezekiel is regularly addressed as "Son of man" may have
contributed to the conception in Enoch.

lions while the Son of man was in heaven would be a minor difficulty to the author of Enoch, if he once seized upon the valid and significant truth (which is the ultimate justification, if not of the form, at least of the substance, of apocalyptic) that there is a genuine continuity between the faithful and suffering people (represented by the prophet Daniel), and the vindicated and glorious people (represented by the Son of man).

We may therefore feel some confidence in reading 1 Enoch 71 as it stands in the manuscripts rather than as it stands in Charles's emended version; and Dr Sjöberg's argument[32] that the Similitudes are early enough to provide part of the background of the gospels and the teaching of Jesus stands, even if they were not in favour with the apocalyptic group at Qumran.[33] Now if we are justified in reading in 1 Enoch the story of an eschatological prophet who was exalted to heaven to be the Son of man, and in taking this to be part of the background of the gospels, its relevance to the thought of Jesus about himself, and to his and the Church's use of the term Son of man, can hardly be doubted. For in the gospels too we encounter one who lives a human life on earth, makes prophecies of the coming reign of God and of the future activities of the heavenly Son of man, and finally is exalted to heaven and there identified with the Son of man. That the Enochic and the gospel developments of the Son of man theme are unrelated does not seem probable, though it is by no means impossible that the latter should be based directly upon Daniel without any literary intermediary; that there is resemblance between Enoch and the gospels is a simple matter of fact.

[32] E. Sjöberg, *Der Menschensohn im äthiopischen Henochbuch*, 1946, pp. 35–9. "So viel ist jedenfalls klar, dass Jesus und die Urgemeinde in einem geistigen Milieu lebten, wo die Vorstellungen vom Menschensohne, die uns in den Bilderreden begegnen, lebendig waren" (p. 39).

[33] M. Burrows, *More Light on the Dead Sea Scrolls*, 1958, pp. 71f.: "The portion containing the Parables or Similitudes ... is not represented by any of the fragments [found at Qumran]. Milik's inference that this was a Christian work of the second century A.D. ... may not win general assent; it may well have been a separate work, however, unknown at Qumran and only later combined with the other parts of the book."

Resemblance; not identity. For (to take only the most important matter) while Enoch was probably chosen as the vehicle of revelation because he did not die but was exalted to heaven, nothing is more central in the gospels than the fact that Jesus did die; and this fact was, it appears, also central in the early preaching. In the gospels, moreover, it is emphasized that it was precisely as Son of man that Jesus died. This is a clear, and was probably a conscious, inversion of the conventional picture of the Son of man. This, however, need not mean that the theme of suffering and humiliation, and the theme of glory, are in truth mutually exclusive, though some apocalyptic writers, actuated by black and white notions of rewards and punishments, may have thought so. We have already seen some coherence between them; the next step is to consider the theological significance of the Son of man title.

"Son of man" means man. If in use it differs at all from the simple word "man" it does so by drawing attention to the generic characteristics of man. But in what sense? Are we speaking of the characteristics of man as he is, or of man as he ought to be, or was created to be? Old Testament usage varies. In Ezekiel the prophet is frequently addressed as "Son of man" in such a way as to bring out his creatureliness; over against God and angels he is mere man. But it is not so in Daniel. Addressed as man, the prophet is placed on a level with angels, and beasts are imported into the imagery to fill a lower role. The beasts of Daniel recall another Old Testament passage, more important for the understanding of "Son of man" than is sometimes recognized.

> When I look at thy heavens, the work of thy fingers,
> The moon and the stars which thou hast established;
> What is man that thou art mindful of him,
> And the son of man that thou dost care for him?
> Yet thou hast made him little less than God,
> And dost crown him with glory and honour.
> Thou hast given him dominion over the works of thy hands;
> Thou hast put all things under his feet,
> All sheep and oxen,

And also the beasts of the field,
The birds of the air, and the fish of the sea,
Whatever passes along the paths of the sea (Ps. 8.4–9).

The Psalm speaks of man as God created him, and as he ideally is, and ought to be. He is only a little lower than God himself, for he bears God's image, and differs from him mainly (though of course very significantly) in that he is creature, whereas God is creator. When he lives in humble and grateful recognition of this fact his true nature, and thus his true greatness, appear, and, small though he is in comparison with the heavens, he is seen as lord of the world, with dominion over all creation.

From this position of humble glory man has fallen away. Desiring to make his dominion more secure he has rebelled against the Creator, and lost the dominion that he had. If he is to be restored it must be by two steps: (1) by a return to humble obedience before God, and (2) by a return to glory and authority. It is evident that the gospels speak of these two stages, for they represent Jesus as living a life of complete trust in and obedience to his Father, drinking to the last drop the cup of suffering that the Father gives him, and they contain the promise of the future glory of the Son of man.

The gospels also speak of Jesus as the Son of man, and since the Son of man is a representative figure we must see his suffering and glory as the suffering and glory of mankind, and as constituting the restoration of mankind to the position for which man was designed by God. It was in this light that Paul (for example) saw Jesus, and if this idea of representation is entertained at all, the idea of the Church is admitted,[34] for it is in a community living in the adverse circumstances of this age that faith and obedience can be realistically expressed. If the suffering of Jesus had been followed immediately by his glory, men would either have been excluded from the glory of the Son of man and the establishing of the kingdom of God in power, or they would have been included without the moral

---

[34] That is, theologically; I am not here discussing the authenticity of passages containing the word ἐκκλησία, or whether Jesus looked forward to the existence of an earthly community.

discipline of living by faith as God's creatures in a disordered world.

It is thus possible, under Paul's guidance, to trace out, by means of the Son of man concept, a theological continuity between the historical Jesus and the Church, which, after its Easter experience, looked both back and up to him as its Lord. What this means, however, is not that one could infer from the teaching of Jesus the future existence of the Church, but that, given the historical existence of Jesus and the Church, it is possible to relate the one to the other.

We must observe, moreover, that the interest and intention of the gospel tradition took a different direction. This began from the identification of the Jesus of history with the heavenly Lord, and proceeded to express this continuity in personal and titular terms, as I have noted above. The same person was the Son of man who lived homeless but authoritative on earth; who suffered and died on behalf of many; who was raised from the dead on the third day; who now reigned in heaven and was to come with the clouds at the end of time. Here the emphasis lies not upon the destiny of mankind, but upon the career and status of Jesus, who expressed his personal dominion by accurately forecasting all that was to happen to him. The more the theological interpretation fixed upon the centrality of Jesus in the destiny of the race as a whole (and of this there is no doubt, at least for Paul), the more inevitable it became that the historical tradition should take this directly, if superficially, Christological tone. But this is not to say that either the theological interpretation or the historical tradition can claim to represent the teaching of Jesus himself; in earlier lectures we have seen reason to think that neither of them does.

This means that we must ask two questions: (1) What did Jesus himself teach about the meaning of his life and death, and about the future? (2) By what steps did this teaching come to be what we now find in the gospels? Our answers to these questions cannot be more than guesses, but unless we are to renounce the duty of historical inquiry we must do the best we can.

1. Jesus, like many another in his day, announced the near

approach of the kingdom of God. He was, however, more than a herald, for he believed that the coming of the kingdom was related to his own teaching and work. This was the secret of the kingdom, a secret which the wise and prudent were disqualified from understanding, for it was contrary to the ordinary principles of wisdom that the glory of God's kingdom should be contingent upon, and adumbrated in, the popular preaching and miracle-working of one who was utterly without recognizable status. Yet for Jesus this was the essence of the matter, and it derived from his understanding of God, which was in line with that of the Old Testament, though not with the legalistic strand[35] in the development of post-biblical Judaism. God's kingdom meant God's grace, the undistinguishing regard of the heavenly Father, which could be grasped only by men who were content to be the Father's little children, and to accept the kingdom as his gift. Any claim to have merited it indicated failure to apprehend the true nature of God's command (which is not satisfied by mere abstention from murder, adultery, and so forth), and failure to apprehend the nature of God himself, as revealed in the mission of Jesus to sinners.

At this point we reach the vital link, which is of supreme importance for an integrated understanding of the teaching of Jesus. The phrase "the kingdom of God" is, as has long been recognized, not the specification of a territory, or an area of human activity, but a proposition about God, who reigns as king. The establishing of the kingdom, however, involves also a proposition about man. Man involved in the kingdom or reign of God is described in the gospels in moral and religious terms. He is, for example, poor in spirit, he mourns, he is meek, he is hungry and thirsty, he is pitiful, pure in heart, a peacemaker, and he rejoices in persecution for Jesus' sake. He may also be collectively determined as "man as he was created to be"; more familiarly, as Son of man. We have noted some of the evidence that Jesus did not seek, and may even have repudiated, some of the honorific titles of Judaism, and that he refused to define the authority with which he acted. But he was

35 See p. 67 and n. 47.

(and this was the ground of the authority which he undoubtedly exercised) the man related to, and expressing, the reign of God; and this meant, man as God made him and willed that he should become: the Son of man.

But not alone. He was to be (in Paul's phrase) the eldest among many brothers. Hence his mission to Israel, and the attempt to reconstitute the people of God, under the grace as well as the command of God. Hence also the undifferentiated predictions (as we have noted them) of suffering for the Son of man. These are essentially true whether the Son of man is conceived individualistically or collectively: it is through many tribulations that men must enter the kingdom of God (Acts 14.22). How far the term Son of man was actually used by Jesus in this connection must remain doubtful. In the pre-Christian apocalypses of Daniel and Enoch no precise earthly role is given to the Son of man, though, as we have seen, he is more or less plainly identified with an earthly prophet and witness, and, so far as he is a representative figure, he represents a suffering people. It is, however, only in glory that he becomes a distinct and differentiated figure. So perhaps it was in the teaching of Jesus (as Mark 8.38 may suggest). At all events, the glorious coming of the Son of man would mean the vindication of those who heard and obeyed the words of Jesus, and were not ashamed to share the fate he incurred. How this vindication would happen mattered little, and Jesus seems to have used the conventional apocalyptic language of resurrection and of *parousia* to describe it; that it would happen he was sure, because it rested upon the faithfulness of God.

2. "Christ died for our sins according to the Scriptures; he was buried; and on the third day he was raised from the dead according to the Scriptures" (1 Cor. 15.3f.). So Paul and his contemporaries believed. Their faith was given this shape less by the teaching of Jesus than by the fact of the resurrection, and the gradual unrolling of time between the resurrection and the *parousia* of the Son of man. The effect of this change of perspective upon the tradition was twofold.

(a) With the lapse of time and the emergence of the Church
as a society living under worldly conditions and limitations, it
became possible to take a clearer view of the relation between
Jesus and the people of God, between the One and the many.
It is not simply that the Church's concerns were read back into
the gospel tradition, though that this happened is undoubtedly
true. The very existence of the Church was brought out in that
it became clear—far clearer than it seems to have been in the
teaching of Jesus—that there was One who did the suffering,
and many who were suffered for. The predictions of suffering
accordingly took clear and differentiated shape: "The Son of
man came to give his life as a ransom in place of many" (Mark
10.45). Not all the predictions were accommodated to this
norm; enough were left untouched to give us an insight into the
uncorrected tradition of Jesus' words. The many were indeed
to suffer in their turn; none knew this better than Mark, who
(we may reasonably guess) had witnessed the martyrdoms of
Peter and Paul, and of others of his Christian brethren. Moreover, it became their vocation to continue the mission of Jesus,
and to extend its scope from the outcasts of Israel to the Gentile
world, though, in the absence of any specific direction from
Jesus, this proved at first no easy step to take. The great
achievement of those who transmitted and edited the gospel
tradition was so to reconstruct the eschatological framework of
the teaching of Jesus as to make room for the continuing
existence of a community between the resurrection and the
coming of the Son of man.[36] It is to their credit as responsible
historians and thinkers that they did this with, on the whole,
minimum disturbance of the original material, being content to
separate corporate suffering from individual, and to distinguish
between the preliminary and private vindication of Jesus given
in his resurrection, and the final and public vindication still to
be made in his coming as the Son of man. Further, this separa-

---

[36] Later, further reconstruction would be called for in order to deal with
the fact that the *parousia* did not take place within the first Christian
generation; but this is a second phase, distinguishable from the first
operation.

tion and this distinction, far-reaching as their effects were, were not made arbitrarily, but in simple recognition of the facts of history. Theological evaluation of the sacrificial efficacy of the death of Jesus, definition of the many for whom Jesus died and of their relation to him and to one another, and prescription of the service they owed him, and of their religious and ethical duties in their unique place "between the times", they were for the most part content to leave to the parallel theological tradition, which we know best in the achievement of Paul.

(b) The gospels were written as part of the activity and self-consciousness of an energetic and expanding society; it is therefore not surprising that (perhaps without any conscious intention on the part of the authors) they reveal a concern to vindicate the place of that society in the purpose of God. The process of definition, however, which we have just noted, has the effect of loosening the figure of Jesus from its Jewish setting and causing him to stand out as the founder of the new religious group,[37] whose person and work equally call for definition. Short of scrapping the old tradition of his words and deeds and starting a new one, it would certainly have been impossible to detach him altogether from Judaism, and such detachment as was achieved was achieved by the use of Jewish tools. Jesus was represented as the foe of all groups within Judaism, demolishing their beliefs, resisting their regulations, and condemning their morals. All this he could rightly do because he was the rightful occupant of all the offices known to the Jewish people: he was himself the coming Son of man, and Messiah, Son of David, and Son of God too. In fact, Jesus in most of his opinions was a Pharisee,[38] and laid claim to no established office. This, however, as we have seen, though true, is not the whole truth. That Jesus exercised authority without defining it made him more, not less, dangerous to established Judaism, and his "blasphemy" was more, not less, deadly because it could not be defined in

[37] This is particularly clear in Luke–Acts; see my *Luke the Historian in Recent Study*, 1961, pp. 58ff.
[38] See p. 62 and n. 43.

8

terms of the regulations. Here too the evangelists and their pre-decessors were not so much falsifying the earlier tradition as defining what had not previously been defined. If it was neces-sary to represent Jesus in conflict with the Pharisees, this had to be done in concrete terms; if Jesus' authority had to be defined, the language of messiahship and of divine sonship was not only inevitable but supported (as we have seen[39]) by genuine traditional material.

There is no satisfactory way of studying the gospel tradition and hunting in it for the teaching of Jesus but the patient process of scrutinizing each verse of the gospels in turn, both by itself and in relation to all possible parallels. This takes a long time, and cannot be done in three lectures. Perhaps, however, the line of investigation we have followed may have done something to show the origins of the tradition in historic fact, and the course by which it came to be what we may read in the gospels. These contain no videographic reproduction of what Jesus said and did; but they do record, in the light of developing history, how God in Christ reconciled the world to himself, and from the new Adam began to build under his own sovereignty the new humanity. And this, it may be, is the most accurate account of the Jesus of history that we could hope, or wish, to have.

[39] See pp. 19–34.

Postscript

In the Preface, I referred to a deficiency in these lectures that was not due (like others) to my own lack of knowledge and ability, but to the terms of the undertaking I had set myself. I cannot hope in this short note to make the deficiency good, but to fail to draw attention to it would be less than honest. There are two points to make; the latter grows out of the former.

1. In these lectures I have dealt with the teaching of the gospels, and, so far as possible, the teaching of Jesus himself, about his own person and mission, his work and his suffering, his hopes and beliefs for the future. To do this has not, I hope, been a waste of time. Yet Jesus did not, except incidentally, teach about himself; rather he drew attention away from himself. This fact accounts for many of the difficulties we have encountered, for these are caused not only by the vicissitudes of the tradition in its transmission, but also by the properties of the material transmitted. This does not mean that the gospels have nothing to offer to the student of Christology or of the Atonement; far from it; but we are not playing fair with them either as historical or as theological sources if we do not follow the gaze of Jesus away from himself and to God. Certainly, it is by looking at Jesus, and by looking through his eyes, that we shall see God, but it is possible to focus one's sight myopically upon Jesus so as to miss the Father whose Son he is. It is true that the

gospels (and the New Testament at large) are Christocentric, but Christ himself is theocentric; or, in the simpler and better language of Paul, "You belong to Christ, and Christ belongs to God" (1 Cor. 3.23). More simply still, "He that has seen me has seen the Father" (John 14.9); only, as the context of these words shows, it is possible to study the history of Jesus at some length without even perceiving that the issue involved in it is the truth about God. It is to this truth that Jesus himself directs us.

What did Jesus teach about God? It is an elementary but important starting-point that he knew and accepted the Old Testament conception of God: God was the Lord—one, holy, mighty, and loving. This conception is given new content and force both by Jesus' ethical teaching and by his eschatological teaching. It is a modest claim, historically, if we start from the belief that Jesus held that he had a unique understanding of the moral demands made on men by God, and that the final working out of God's purpose for mankind was in some way connected with his mission. These propositions may be accepted independently of the historicity of any particular saying, since apart from them the story as a whole does not make sense. A postscript is no place to work out their significance for man's understanding of God; and the task has been done far better than I could do it by Rudolf Bultmann, from whom I shall allow myself one quotation.

> Thus it has finally become clear in what sense God is for Jesus God of the present and of the future. God is God of the present, because His claim confronts man in the present moment, and He is at the same time God of the future, because He gives man freedom for the present instant of decision, and sets before him as the future which is opened to him by his decision, condemnation or mercy. God is God of the present for the sinner precisely because He casts him into remoteness from Himself, and He is at the same time God of the future because He never relinquishes His claim on the sinner and opens to him by forgiveness a new future for new obedience.[1]

[1] *Jesus and the Word*, 1935, p. 211. Cf. also §3 of Bultmann's *Theologie des Neuen Testaments*.

In this postscript I shall briefly develop the doctrine of God only in terms of the subjects discussed in the lectures. This leads to the second point.

2. Jesus' primary concern was not to define or publicize himself, but to point to God and speak his word. The significance of this has been sharpened by our historical study. For, if the historical analysis conducted in these lectures is right, Jesus was wrong—not simply mistaken in thinking that Moses wrote the Pentateuch and David the Psalms, but mistaken in major matters. He believed that his disciples would suffer with him, and they did not. He believed that suffering would be immediately followed, or even interrupted, by a divine act of vindication that would establish the kingdom of God and bring world history to a close; but though his disciples became convinced that he himself had come to life again, and were in consequence transformed men, the world continued in the old way: the sun was not darkened, nor the moon turned into blood. Jesus was mistaken, and since the things he looked for did not happen he died with the disillusioned avowal that God had forsaken him. But again he was mistaken: God had not forsaken him.

Christian theology has, understandably, been slow to acknowledge these errors, but they emerge clearly enough from historical study of the gospels. At first sight, they appear to suggest that the story of Jesus may be safely ignored, like that of any other deluded enthusiast. But it is precisely at this point that the difference between Jesus and all deluded enthusiasts demands recognition. They call attention to themselves, and therefore stand or fall with their ability to convince others of the truth of their own claims and the security of their own position. Jesus did not make claims for himself, nor was he in the least interested in his own security. The end of the story was a fulfilment, more precise and radical than he himself had expected, of what he himself had taught. I am not referring here to the "predictions of the passion" (which have been discussed in Lecture 2); even if all of these should prove to be *vaticinia ex eventu* it remains true that Jesus refused to press any claim for himself or his authority, and taught the way of sacrificial obedience to God, confident that God, who cared for the fall of a sparrow, would not suffer even a hair to perish from the head of his elect. Jesus was right, in being mistaken. But paradoxes of this kind demand immediate sober explanation. Two points may be made here.

(*a*) If, in some matters, particularly in his sense of eschatological perspective, Jesus was in error, God was not. It was the total event, beginning with the ministry of Jesus and ending with the "delay of the *parousia*", that constituted the redemptive act of God in history. The whole story is full of thwarted and redirected plans. This is true of the course of the ministry, for (to take an outstanding example) whatever we make of passages such as Mark 4.10ff. we can scarcely doubt that Jesus set out on his public ministry with the intention of convincing his hearers of the truth of what he was saying; we can scarcely think that he made up parable after parable, murmuring with satisfaction, "*That* will prevent them from getting any idea what I am talking about." Yet this was the effect of his teaching. Israel heard, but did not believe, and not believing did not understand. Again, it is difficult to believe that Jesus called disciples with the clear intention that one of them should betray, another deny, and the rest desert him. Yet this is what happened. So far however it is not difficult to understand the process, now that it lies behind us in history. The message had to be presented to Israel in the way it was, and not (as Paul was later to say) in persuasive words of wisdom, in order that the response might rest, and might be seen to rest, on faith only, and not on human cleverness. The disciples had to be broken, that their faith might rest, and might be seen to rest, upon the power of God, and not on their own steadfastness. The ministry ended, as Jesus foretold, in suffering. This theme has perhaps been sufficiently discussed. It too involved a reversal of human standards, judgements, and preconceived opinions, in which truth (the truth, for example, of Jesus' royal authority), which could have been brought out in no other way, was revealed.

So much for the ministry, and its shadowed end. May not the reinterpretation of Jesus' eschatology, and the "delay of the *parousia*", be understood similarly? It is natural that men should wish to see without delay the happy ending of the story in which they are involved; natural also that those who experienced events so profoundly disturbing as the death and resurrection of Jesus should suppose that any subsequent extension of history could be nothing but an anti-climax. But may it not have been God's intention, unforeseen in its full extent even by Jesus himself, that life between the incarnation and the *parousia* should be the normal state of mankind? In this way men, caught in the tension of deferred hope but living by the Holy Spirit, might learn the discipline of the life of the children of God, each generation wrestling afresh with fear and defeat, existing under the shadow of death, and discovering what it is to live by faith. How could the discovery be made in any other setting? *Vivendo, immo moriendo et damnando fit theologus, non intelligendo, legendo, aut speculando. Fit Christianus*, Luther might have written.[2] If it be true that the significance of Jesus is seen most clearly in the crucifixion, we may reasonably conclude that God sees more usefulness in allowing mankind a long period in which to bear the cross after his Son (not merely in suffering, but in the darkness of rejected service and love, of motives misunderstood, of disillusionment and despair), than in providing immediate glory for an undisciplined company of the elect. Here too natural human expectation had to be negated.

(*b*) If this proposition is true, its truth is rooted in the truth about God, and it was the truth about God, rather than historical and apocalyptic timetables, that Jesus was concerned to proclaim. I have already pointed out that our difficulty in digging history out of the gospels is due not only to the corruption of the tradition but also to the fact that the material of the tradition itself is not interested in the niceties of accurate narra-

---

[2] "It is not thinking, reading, or speculating, but living, yes, dying and being damned, that make a theologian", said Luther. For "theologian" he might have said "Christian".

tive; it is interested in God. In other words, the centre of gravity in Jesus' teaching lay in God, and in the relation of men to God. It is true that he saw his own ministry as constituting a crisis in God's dealings with men; for this reason the actual course of events in which he was engaged is of fundamental importance, and the historical study of the gospels is not merely justified but imperative. But the God whose final envoy Jesus was, was also the God who had commissioned Moses and the prophets; there was no other than he, and though he acted in history his actions were indicative of, and arose out of, his essential and eternal being. It was because he was the sort of God Jesus declared him to be, and desired to be related to men in the sovereignty of grace, that Jesus foresaw obedient suffering, followed by vindication, as his own role in the task of making God known, and renewing man's relation with his Creator. He would incorporate in himself the loving initiative of God in re-establishing his sovereignty, and the loving response of man in accepting it and its implications. It turned out that the suffering was more acute than the human Jesus had foreseen: despair, disillusionment, and defeat mix a more bitter cup than heroic resistance, and death in a mistaken cause robs even the martyr of his dying satisfaction. And the vindication was extended and deepened in a way beyond the human imagination of Jesus: it was the Father's will to bring many sons, not one, and not one generation only, into glory. But the very fact that Jesus' human estimates fell so far short of the facts did more to prove him right in principle than an exact fulfilment in a dispute begun and ended in the Sanhedrin—a fate, perhaps, like Stephen's—could have done.

By being mistaken in detail, Jesus was more effectively shown to be right in all that really mattered than he could have been by small-scale accuracy. At the same time, he was shown to be very man, subject to our infirmity. Perhaps this is why, not least when we study the gospels with the most stringent historical discipline, he speaks to us as the word of God, in our speech.

Indexes

1. BIBLICAL REFERENCES

2. OTHER REFERENCES

3. MODERN AUTHORS

4. NAMES AND SUBJECTS

Some subjects (notably "Son of man") are referred to so frequently as to make it unprofitable to record them in an Index.